HEMINGWAY IN ITALY

Hemingway in Italy

Richard Owen

This first paperback edition published in 2020

Published in Great Britain in 2017 by
The Armchair Traveller
4 Cinnamon Row
London SW11 3TW
www.hauspublishing.com

A CIP record for this book is available from the British Library

ISBN: 978-1-909961-70-8
eISBN: 978-1-909961-41-8

Typeset in Garamond by MacGuru Ltd

Printed and bound in the UK by TJ International, Padstow

Contents

Acknowledgements and Sources

I AM INDEBTED to a number of people in Venice and the Veneto who helped me to research this book and granted me interviews: Irina Ivancich (Marchesi), daughter of Gianfranco and Cristina Ivancich and hence Adriana's niece, who showed me not only the Villa Mocenigo-Baggiani-Ivancich at San Michele al Tagliamento and the family's Palazzo Rota-Ivancich in Venice but also many of the places linked to Hemingway in and around Monastier; Baron Alberto Franchetti, who shared with me his boyhood memories of Hemingway and explained the finer points of duck hunting; Ciccinella Kechler, who introduced me to Hemingway enthusiasts at the Villa Barbarigo-De Aserta-Kechler at Fraforeano; Bruno Marcuzzo, the Hemingway guide at Fossalta di Piave, whose tour can be found on the website www.laguerradihemingway.it/percorso.html; Alberto Luca, Giandomenico Cortese and Raffaela Mocellin at the Fondazione Luca's 'Hemingway and the Great War' museum at Bassano del Grappa; and Ivano Sartor, former mayor of Roncade and now the town's archivist and historian.

My thanks at Ca' Foscari, Venice University, to Professor Valerio de Scarpis, Professor Rosella Mamoli Zorzi, Professor Emeritus Sergio Perosa and Associate Professor Gregory Dowling for their advice and insights; and at Oxford University to Martin McLaughlin, Professor of Italian and Italian Studies, and the staff of the Bodleian Library.

My thanks, too, to Consuelo Ivancich at the Villa Mocenigo; Donatella Asta (née Kechler); Baron Vincenzo Ciani Bassetti and his family and staff at the Castello di Roncade; the staff of the Park Hotel Villa Fiorita at Monastier for the exhibition 'Hemingway + Piave' at the villa, curated by local historian Angelo Ceron; Davide Lorigliola for his expertise on Hemingway and Friuli; and Massimo Sensini, the mayor of Fossalta di Piave. I am grateful to Clara Noli for making available to me her 2008 dissertation at Genoa University, 'Adriana Ivancich a Venezia: Alterita e integrazione di una scrittrice', and to Richard Ward and Justine Taylor of the Honourable Artillery Company for information on the Battle of the Piave.

Films made about Hemingway include: *My Name is Ernest*, directed by Emilio Briguglio, with Massimiliano Tondello as Hemingway, Eleonora Bolla as Agnes and Anita Kravos as Adriana (2014); *Hemingway and Gellhorn*, an HBO made-for-TV movie starring Clive Owen as Hemingway and Nicole Kidman as Martha Gellhorn, directed by Philip Kaufman (2012); *Michael Palin's Hemingway Adventure*, BBC, four episodes (1999); *Ernest Hemingway: Wrestling with Life*, directed by Stephen Crisman and narrated by Mariel Hemingway, US documentary (1998); and *In Love and War*, directed by Richard Attenborough, with Chris O'Donnell as Hemingway and Sandra Bullock as Agnes (1997).

I have drawn on the biographies and studies of Hemingway in English and Italian listed in the Bibliography, and on the three volumes of Hemingway's collected letters published by Cambridge University Press, as well as the *Selected Letters 1917–1961* edited by Carlos Baker. The writer's archive of letters, manuscripts and photographs, donated by his wife Mary, is held in the Hemingway Collection at the Kennedy Library in Boston, Massachusetts. Some scholars regard AE Hotchner's memoirs as not altogether reliable. On the other hand, as Linda Patterson Miller points out in the Spring 2016 edition of *The Hemingway Review*, they "ring true" emotionally and deal with "a pivotal time in Hemingway's life that would inspire thereafter the predominant themes of his art – betrayal, remorse and possible redemption through art".

My thanks to Ilse and Barbara Schwepcke at Haus Publishing, and to Emma Henderson, my editor at Haus; to the Hemingway Foundation and Society; to Yessenia Santos, Senior Permissions Manager at Simon and Schuster, and the Hemingway Foreign Rights Trust; and to Mark Cirino, Associate Professor of English and the Melvin M. Peterson Endowed Chair of English at Evansville University, Indiana, and General Editor of the *Reading Hemingway* series for Kent State University Press.

My greatest debts are to the late Giovanni Cecchin, former visiting lecturer at Princeton, whose detailed and indefatigable research into Hemingway and Italy over a period of twenty years is an indispensable resource; and to my wife Julia, who accompanied me on my travels and whose knowledge of Italy was invaluable as ever.

There are some misunderstandings concerning Hemingway's Italian experiences: the Milan American Red Cross hospital where Hemingway was treated, and where he fell in love with Agnes, was in Via Cesare Cantu, not Via Manzoni; Jim Gamble, Hemingway's superior in the mobile canteen service at the front, was not a member of the Procter and Gamble soap dynasty; Elsie Jessup, Agnes von Kurowsky's fellow nurse and partial model for Catherine Barkley, was American, not English; the foreign minister Hemingway and Guy Hickok visited in San Marino in 1927 was not Mussolini but almost certainly Giuliano Gozi. I may of course have made errors of my own; if so, they are the responsibility of none of the above but mine alone.

Introduction

"Sometimes I think we only half live over here. The Italians live all the way"

> Hemingway to his sister Marcelline after his
> return from the Italian front in 1919

E RNEST HEMINGWAY is most often associated with Chicago, Florida, 1920s Paris, Spain, Cuba and Africa. But Italy was equally important in his life and work: it gave him his first brush with war at the Austrian front in the First World War (*A Farewell to Arms*), provided him with inspiration after the Second World War (*Across the River and Into the Trees*), and helped him to recuperate after he was seriously injured in two plane crashes while on safari in Africa in the 1950s.

It was also the country in which he met the first great love of his life, Agnes von Kurowsky, and the last, Adriana Ivancich – the two women for whom he felt overwhelming passion, Agnes when he was not yet twenty, Adriana when he was fifty. Ironically both relationships – as far as we know – were platonic; he had four marriages and a number of affairs, but Agnes and Adriana were for Hemingway not just objects of desire, they were idealised visions of the eternal feminine which captivated him, one at the outset of his action-packed life, the other as it neared its final phase.

He started out not as a novelist, but as a journalist and foreign correspondent. I had long admired Hemingway's fiction; when I had the idea for this book after visiting Bassano del Grappa, and started to look into his links with Italy, I found that among the many Hemingway works I already had on my bookshelves were the collected *Nick Adams Stories* and a first edition of *Across the River and Into the Trees*. But what also drew me to him was the fact that his fiction is underpinned by the thorough research and memory for detail which is (or should be) part of the craft of journalism.

He did not keep notes or a journal, he once told his friend and assistant Aaron (AE) Hotchner: he could "just push the recall button and there it is". The spare and direct minimalist writing style for which he became famous – and which influenced a generation of writers – was first crafted on the *Kansas City Star*, whose style guide instructed reporters to use short sentences and simple, vigorous language. Hemingway later served as European correspondent for the *Toronto Star*, covering among other dramas the Greco-Turkish war and meeting Benito Mussolini, both before and after he became Italy's dictator.

He led and described a life of action, from bull fighting and deep-sea fishing to big game hunting on safaris. When his early collection of short stories *Men Without Women* was published in 1927 some reviewers said he was fundamentally a reporter preoccupied with bull fighters, bruisers, touts, gunmen, soldiers, prostitutes, hard drinkers and dope fiends. Like DH Lawrence, whom he admired, he has tended to be seen in our own time as unfashionably misogynist. As Caroline Moorehead notes in her biography of Martha Gellhorn, his third wife, his name evokes "masculine swagger", even "an increasingly drunken slide into belligerence and depression". According to his first wife, Hadley Richardson, even his sexual prowess was exaggerated: he was often "too distracted to be a consistently good lover".

His excessive drinking was legendary. I am indebted to Gregory

Dowling of Venice University for pointing out that in *Across the River and Into the Trees*, Hemingway's alter ego Colonel Cantwell and his Venetian girlfriend Renata consume "1 gin and campari, 1 double-dry Martini, 2 more dry Martinis, 1 Campari gin and soda and 4 more dry Martinis at Harry's Bar, followed by 1 bottle of Capri Bianco, 1 bottle of Valpolicella, 2 bottles of Champagne (Brut '42) during the meal, another bottle in the gondola, and a bottle of Valpolicella in the hotel room". Professor Dowling adds that this surely "takes us a little beyond the bounds of literary realism" – though it undoubtedly reflects Hemingway's real-life attachment to alcohol.

By the time of his final stay at the Gritti Palace Hotel in Venice in the 1950s, he was drinking Valpolicella at breakfast followed by martinis, daiquiris, tequila and both Scotch and Bourbon whisky. As early as December 1925 he told a friend from Michigan, Bill Smith, that he had done some "A1 drinking" with Pauline Pfeiffer, the *Vogue* magazine journalist who would shortly become his second wife. On one occasion he downed two bottles of Beaune with her, followed by a bottle of Chambertin and a bottle of Pommard, plus (though with some help from his fellow writer John Dos Passos) a quart of Haig whisky and "a quart of hot Kirsch". He claimed he had "never been fitter" and rose every morning with a clear head and "in absolutely swell shape".

"I notice you speak slightingly of the bottle", he wrote to his Russian translator Ivan Kashkin in August 1935. "I have drunk since I was fifteen and few things have given me more pleasure." Rum was best to steady the nerves before an attack, whisky for keeping out the cold, red wine essential with food. But in reality he suffered (not surprisingly) from chronic liver and kidney problems as well as high blood pressure. He was also accident prone, forever injuring himself sailing, driving, skiing or on safari, and at one stage in Paris brought a glass bathroom skylight down on his head by pulling the wrong chain, causing gashes which required nine stitches.

And yet, Caroline Moorehead adds, "for a whole generation, the 'lost generation' whose malaise he so perfectly captured, he was regarded by many as the finest writer of his age." Hemingway, Anthony Burgess wrote, was "six-feet-tall, huge-chested, handsome, ebullient, a warrior, a hunter, a fisherman, a drinker. It is the fusion of sensitive and original artist and big-muscled man of action that has made of Ernest Hemingway one of the large international myths of the twentieth century." As Hadley's biographer Gioia Diliberto has noted, he disliked "professional beauties and overgroomed social-ites", preferring "strong, intelligent women" who were "not slaves to conventional ideas of femininity".

Orson Welles, who went duck shooting with him near Venice, observed that although in his writing Hemingway was "tense and solemn" in pursuit of what was "true and good", in person he could often be "riotously funny". He could be snobbish and arrogant: Baron Alberto Franchetti, who as a boy went duck hunting with Hemingway on the family estate near Venice in the 1950s, remembers his father, Nanuk, admonishing the writer for distributing sweets to local children from his limousine, telling him "You are not in Africa now". Franchetti also remembers Hemingway standing up and challenging the dozen or so other hunters dining with him to knock him down if they could: "They all ran the length of the room and thumped him on the chest with both hands joined together – but he stayed on his feet and went back to his place smiling and happy with his chest puffed out."

Franchetti nonetheless recalls that Hemingway was "very affec-tionate towards me, a lovely person". For Fernanda Pivano, his Italian translator, the image of Hemingway as "macho" was a "distortion": in reality he was generous to a fault to others (to Ezra Pound, to John Dos Passos, to Gianfranco Ivancich, Adriana's brother), was vulnerable, even fragile beneath his blustering exterior, and had a "timid, disarming smile". Almost all his books, Pivano suggested, were founded on "the struggle between good and evil, in which evil is represented by cowardice and falsity and good is represented by loyalty and courage".

Hemingway, Gianfranco thought, was by nature rather shy and diffident behind his bluff exterior, and was extraordinarily sensitive toward others, seeing their strengths and defects "almost as if he had a sixth sense". "The more our friendship grew", AE Hotchner wrote in his recent memoir *Hemingway in Love*, "the more I realized that the stories that had circulated about his gruff, pugnacious personality were a myth invented by people who didn't know him but judged him by the subjects he wrote about."

Countess Roberta Kechler, the daughter of Federico Kechler, who first introduced Hemingway to hunting in the Veneto, remembers his courage in the face of pain when he returned to the region for the last time after the air crashes in Africa. "He was our guest at our estate at San Martino di Codroipo in Friuli for ten days or so while he recovered: the doctors were astonished that he was still alive. But he loved to say 'I am a fighter'. He was the most generous of beings, generous with his time, and with his intelligence."

Hemingway wrote sensitively and passionately about love and death against an Italian backdrop – and it was above all Venice and the Veneto which he came to regard as his second home. It was here that he developed and honed the spare, clear, uncluttered style of carefully chosen words and phrases for which he became famous, and which has been much imitated since. As Ford Madox Ford noted, "His words strike you, each one, as if they were pebbles fetched fresh from a brook. They live and shine, each in its place." Or as Hemingway himself put it in his memoir *A Moveable Feast*, the task of any writer trying to get started is to write "one true sentence, and then go on from there".

Setting out on his writing career as a young man in Paris, he absorbed the authors whose books he borrowed or bought from

Sylvia Beach's left-bank library and bookshop, including Turgenev, Dostoyevsky and Stendhal as well as contemporaries such as Aldous Huxley – and Lawrence, telling Gertrude Stein that although he could not get on with *Women in Love* he had admired and learned from *Sons and Lovers*, *The White Peacock* and stories such as 'The Prussian Officer'. The admiration was mutual. Lawrence wrote of Hemingway's early collection of stories *In Our Time* that it was "a series of successive sketches from a man's life ... it does not pretend to be about one man. But it is. It is as much as we need know of the man's life. The sketches are short, sharp, vivid, and most of them excellent."

And like Lawrence, Hemingway fell in love with all things Italian, including the language, although he never fully mastered it and often mangled it ("I could never spell Italian and have no diction-ary", he wrote to his editor at Scribner's, Maxwell Perkins, in 1926 when sending the manuscript of his story 'In Another Country'). It was "in the Veneto that my grandfather became a man and experi-enced for the first time the essential things of life – pain and fear in war, and then love and loss, all of which set in motion his fiction", the writer's grandson John Hemingway told the Venice newspaper *Il Gazzettino* in July 2015, during a centenary celebration of Hem-ingway's Italian experiences held at Caorle.

Italian references even worked their way into the original version in 1931 of *Death in the Afternoon*, which is otherwise about Spain, and had to be excised. "They say everyone loves Italy once and that it is well to go through it young", Hemingway said in the original version, adding "I loved northern Italy like a fool, truly, the way I had loved northern Michigan". He listed the places which had cap-tured his heart: Fiesole, Taormina, Rapallo, Milan, Brescia, Verona, Vicenza, Mestre, Treviso, "all around the Venetian plain" and "all of the Dolomites".

It was, above all, the north of Italy that he "really cared about",

Hemingway said. In addition to the Veneto Hemingway remembered most fondly Milan, where his first serious love affair with a Red Cross nurse inspired *A Farewell to Arms*. It was northern Italy which gave him his first taste of freedom, of passion, of companionship under fire, perhaps too of liberty from the Protestant constrictions of the American heartland in which he had grown up.

Some thirty years later he wrote *Across the River and Into the Trees*, a novel which has its faults, as Burgess noted, yet which pays "eloquent homage to Venice" matched by few other works of fiction. Hemingway, Burgess said, evokes Venice's stone and waters, "the views of Torcello and Murano from the lagoon, the cold mornings, the shops and the market", to the point where you can practically taste the city of the sea.

Hemingway came to share not only the Italian love of food, wine, landscape and art but also the attitudes and assumptions which underlie Mediterranean culture, even converting – or so he claimed – to Roman Catholicism. As Rena Sanderson has observed, for Hemingway Italy was forever the land where he could recapture a time when he was "young, handsome and gifted, and for the first time knew war and love – and when life was so full of surprises, promises and great expectations, it may have seemed like heaven on earth".

Writing a story about the war in 1919, Hemingway had his hero declare: "But did you ever see a sunrise from Mount Grappa or know the feel of a June twilight in the Dolomites? Or taste the Strega they have in Cittadella? Or walk through Vicenza at night under a bombing moon? There's a lot to war beside fighting you know." The thoughts are expressed by his character, Pickles McCarty, but surely also reflect his own as he recalls the perfume of "those big purple flowers" hanging over the white walls and walking "in the moonlight down to the trattoria".

It was Italy where Hemingway first fell in love, and Italy where he first faced the very real danger of death. He returned to it again and again, insisting on showing both his first wife, Hadley, and Mary, his fourth and last, the landscapes of his youth. He would surely have agreed wholeheartedly with the French novelist George Sand, who wrote that "Just on the point of leaving Italy, I begin to get acclimatised to it. I shall come again, for having once tasted of that country, one feels as though expelled from Paradise."

1

War in the Dolomites

"I'm an old Veneto boy myself. I love it and know it quite well"
Hemingway to Bernard Berenson

HEMINGWAY IS STILL REMEMBERED in Venice today for his famous frequenting of Harry's Bar, the Rialto and the Locanda Cipriani on the island of Torcello, and for his long association with the Hotel Gritti Palace, where he adopted scampi and Valpolicella as the "ideal cure" while recovering there from injuries sustained on safari in Africa.

But it was the Venice region, the Veneto, which Hemingway experienced first, at the age of just eighteen, as a land and people caught up in the tragic, exhausting final days of the First World War. The Veneto, in the northeast of Italy, is bordered to the west by Lombardy, to the east by Friuli Venezia Giulia, and to the south by Emilia-Romagna, while in the north it meets the South Tyrol – formerly part of Austria, now Trentino-Alto Adige – and Austria itself.

It offers an enchanting and varied landscape, from the mountains of the north with their forests, peaks and waterfalls to the flat coastal plains and the soft green hills and vineyards around Treviso, Padua, Vicenza and Verona. Today we think of the Veneto as the land of Palladian villas, of great painters – Titian, Giorgione, Bellini, Veronese

– and of world-famous wines – Prosecco, Soave, Bardolino, Pinot Grigio, Valpolicella – all against a backdrop of stunning natural beauty, from the Dolomites to the Po Valley, Lake Garda and the Venetian lagoons.

But a hundred years ago the Veneto was the scene of some of the fiercest fighting of the First World War along the 400-mile Italian front. When war broke out in August 1914, Italy was at least nominally a member of the Triple Alliance together with Germany and Austro-Hungary. It did not take part however, arguing that the Alliance was meant to be defensive. In fact Italy harboured long-held resentment against Austro-Hungary, which had taken control of several regions in Italy as part of the 1815 Congress of Vienna peace accord following the Napoleonic Wars.

Well aware of this, British and French politicians secretly persuaded Italy to change sides at the 1915 Treaty of London, signed by the Italian Foreign Minister, Sidney Sonnino. In their repeated offensives, known as the eleven battles of the Isonzo River, the Italians outnumbered their foes (and former allies) by three to one, at least at first, but failed to make gains, apart from capturing Gorizia. The Italian army had suffered from losses of equipment and ammunition in its campaign in Libya three years earlier, but also from low troop morale, with many soldiers distrustful of their army commander, General Luigi Cadorna.

The weather in the "mountain war" was often atrocious: soldiers were killed as much by avalanches as by gunfire or shells. Several times in two years of fighting Italian forces broke through Austrian lines but were forced to withdraw because their supply lines were inadequate. Meanwhile the Austrians were given a boost by the arrival of German reinforcements, and in October 1917 the battered Italians were decisively defeated at the battle of Caporetto, a name which echoes down the years to this day as a symbol of national humiliation.

The Caporetto disaster (the backdrop to *A Farewell to Arms*) gave rise to the myth that the Italian troops lacked the will to fight, and were even cowards. As Spencer di Scala notes in his biography of the wartime Italian prime minister Vittorio Orlando however, although there were cases of mutiny and desertion "Italy's military effort hardly deserves the dismissals its received from its allies after the conflict".

The myth can be traced, he suggests, to the tendency of General Cadorna to blame his troops for setbacks which in fact were due to his own incompetence. Certainly Hemingway later described Italian troops as "the bravest troops in the Allied armies" whose fighting in the impassable mountains deserved "all the credit in the world".

By the time the young Hemingway volunteered to drive Red Cross ambulances at the front, the Italians had retreated to last-ditch defensive lines near Venice. Now, however, it was the turn of the Austrians to founder because their rapid advance had outstripped their supply lines, and Italy's turn to be reinforced by troops from Britain and France. British forces included the 2nd Battalion Honourable Artillery Company (HAC), which among other feats played a crucial role in the surrender of the Austrian garrison at the river island of Papadopoli. Italy also benefited from the help of the United States, which supplied Italy with badly needed strategic materials such as coal and steel.

In what went down in history as the Battle of the Piave River, the Austrians – now deserted by their German allies, who in the Spring of 1918 were under pressure on the Western Front – mounted a two-pronged offensive, only to find that thanks to information given to them by Austrian deserters, the Italians were waiting for them. In October 1918, under a new commander, General Armando Diaz, Italy launched its own offensive across the Piave, crushing the Austrians at Vittorio Veneto. Austro-Hungary sued for peace, and an armistice was signed at Padua in November. It was the beginning of the end of the Austro-Hungarian Empire.

Hemingway only became involved in the war a few months before it ended – but the experience was so profound it stayed with him for the rest of his life. The United States finally entered the war in April 1917, and American engagement in this far-away conflict captured the imagination of a teenager whose boyhood interests had hitherto been closer to home – fishing, hunting and camping in the lakeside woods of northern Michigan.

He was born on 21 July 1899 in Oak Park, a leafy middle-class Chicago suburb: his father, Clarence Edward (known as Ed), was a doctor, and his mother, Grace, was a musician, singer and artist. They were a church-going family (Ernest had four sisters and a younger brother), with a summer home on Walloon Lake, near Petoskey, Michigan, which gave the young Hemingway his life-long love of the outdoors.

At high school in Oak Park he excelled at boxing, athletics and water polo. But his other passion was English, and the school newspaper, *The Trapeze*, in 1916 published his first piece, about a local performance by the Chicago Symphony Orchestra of Bach, Brahms and Wagner: no doubt with advice from his mother he used surprisingly professional musical terms ("excellent staccato work", "smoothly flowing motif"). In high school he also began to write stories, including 'The Judgement of Manitou', in which a Michigan Indian hunter who has falsely accused his white companion of stealing shoots himself after stepping into a bear trap, reflecting that this is the fate decreed by Manitou, an Indian god.

Impatient to be a proper writer, Hemingway decided to forego college and instead head straight into journalism. Thanks to an uncle who lived in Kansas City and knew the chief editorial writer on the *Kansas City Star* he spent a six-month stint as a trainee local reporter on the paper, where he studied the style book diligently to acquire the house style of "vigorous English" and "short sentences" while "not forgetting to strive for smoothness".

But the young trainee also longed for adventure: he was fascinated by military history, especially the American Civil War, in which both his maternal grandfather Ernest Hall (born in Sheffield) and his paternal grandfather Anson Hemingway had fought. The chance for action came in the form of the American Red Cross, which was recruiting ambulance drivers for the Italian front. He had already volunteered for the Missouri Home Guard: now came the prospect of adventure abroad.

Hemingway may have been influenced by Hugh Walpole, the English writer who at the outbreak of war in 1914 had been rejected for army service because of poor eyesight and had instead enlisted in the Russian Red Cross, an experience he described in his novel *The Dark Forest*, which the young Hemingway had read (and in which the hero falls in love with a nurse). Hemingway later claimed that, like Walpole, he had applied for army service but been turned down because of an eye defect (he had a weakness in his left eye), although biographers have found no record of such an application.

Whatever the truth, toward the end of May 1918, after rejecting the offer of a safer job away from the frontline dealing with logistics, he found himself sailing on a battered French transport ship called – appropriately enough – the *Chicago* ("a rotten old tub") from New York to Bordeaux. He and other volunteers went to Paris, which at the time was under bombardment from German artillery, and finally reached Milan in early June, lodging in some style not at a hostel but at the Hotel Vittoria near the city centre. Before leaving the US the American Red Cross had given the newly recruited drivers the rank of second lieutenant and issued them with US army officer uniforms.

To this Hemingway, who thought the uniform looked "like a million dollars", added stylish cordovan (or cordwain) leather boots and later a Sam Browne belt. His first duty was distinctly unglamorous on the other hand: in a baptism of fire (his own words),

Hemingway was sent on his first day in Milan to a bombed munitions factory at Bollate, twelve miles from the city, to collect the bodies of female workers, an episode he later described in *Death in the Afternoon*. "One becomes so accustomed to all the dead being men that the sight of a dead woman is quite shocking", he wrote.

The grisly scene he found was in stark contrast to the "pleasant, though dusty, ride through the beautiful Lombard countryside": arriving where the munitions plant had been, "some of us were put to patrolling about those large stocks of munitions which for some reason had not exploded, while others were put at extinguishing a fire which had gotten into the grass of an adjacent field".

They were then ordered to pick the charred remains of the dead women off the surrounding barbed-wire fence and take them to an improvised mortuary. What struck Hemingway most forcibly was the fact that some of the women's long hair had been completely burned away. "I remember that after we had searched quite thoroughly for the complete dead we collected fragments."

Back in Milan, Hemingway and his equally novice Red Cross colleagues tried to come to terms with this "unreal" experience, and dealt with it by being detached, analysing (as he put it) the way a human body could be "blown into pieces which exploded along no anatomical lines but rather divided as capriciously as the fragmentation in the burst of a high explosive shell". There was also time for his first taste of a city he would get to know better shortly – the Duomo, the cafes of the adjacent Vittorio Emmanuele Gallery, the San Siro race track.

But within a few days he was at the Italian front where, as he later wrote, the 18-year-old Hemingway lost forever "the illusion of immortality". Italy was "the strongest experience of his youth, the one that made him a man and the writer we know", says Angelo Ceron, curator of an exhibition marking the centenary of the First World War at Villa Fiorita, in Monastier di Treviso, which at the time was on the frontline. "He arrived in Italy from the States full of ideals, a non-drinker and pure, and during his stay in the Veneto he lived through very powerful and shocking experiences: war, death, love and alcohol."

Some insights into the Venice and Veneto of the time can be gleaned from the letters of Hemingway's fellow novelist John Dos Passos, who had also volunteered as an ambulance driver and was at first stationed at Dolo, ten miles from Venice. In January 1918 he described going on a "little steamer" through the "cold lagoon water" from Fusina to Venice, only to find the city "swathed in sandbags", the elaborately carved front of the Doges Palace "bricked up for fear of aero bombs", shops and shutters closed, windows boarded up and the city inhabited by soldiers and sailors "and a few scared civilians". And yet "there was enough life left in it to excite me considerably".

The flat landscape of the Piave district is today a mixture of farmland, vineyards, housing estates and light industries. What was once a battlefield is now bisected by the Venice-Trieste motorway. But the villas Hemingway discovered are still there, as are the canals and the straight roads lined with plane trees, and the Dolomites looming above. It is not difficult to recapture the mixture of excitement and enchantment the young Hemingway felt as he arrived in what had been transformed from a placid agricultural area into a war zone.

The first American ambulance drivers had arrived toward the end of 1917, and were divided into five sections: No 1 at Bassano del Grappa, No 2 at Roncade, No 3 first at Dolo then at Casale sul Sile, No 4 at Schio and No 5 at Fanzolo. Hemingway was assigned on 9 June 1918 to Schio, below Mount Pasubio, southeast of Rovereto and north of Vicenza, where the Section IV unit drove battleship-grey ambulances with a red cross painted on the roof and sides.

Hemingway and his fellow volunteers (many of them students from Harvard) were housed in a former wool warehouse by a stream, the 30,000-square-metre Lanificio Cazzola, with the upper floor once used to store wool lined with army camp beds, with a trunk at the foot of each one and a giant stars and stripes hanging from the ceiling. A plaque on the building – now converted into apartments – records in both Italian and English the gratitude of local people to Hemingway and the other Section IV drivers for their "work of human solidarity".

Hemingway also found time to write for the Schio Red Cross newsletter, called *Ciao*. The mess or canteen on the ground floor, run by the Italian army, offered spaghetti, rabbit stew and local wine: when off duty the volunteer drivers enjoyed even better fare at an inn in the town centre, the Albergo Due Spade in Via Carducci, where Hemingway had first lodged – now a charming *osteria* with a stone plaque on the frontage portraying Hemingway – or drank beer at the Stella d'Italia and the Alla Fraschetta. Another favourite haunt was the Osteria Madonnetta ('Little Madonna') in the picturesque town of Marostica, situated between Schio and Bassano del Grappa, home to another Red Cross ambulance base.

Little more than a decade old at the time (it was founded in 1904) the Madonetta still has the same tables and chairs, according to the present owner, Wladimir Guerra. "My grandmother Amelia remembered the Americans who came here – in fact they came so often we were known as the *Osteria degli Americani*. She said they mostly drank – there was not much to eat, and in those days you had to bring your own bread to go with the wine."

Hemingway must have been enchanted by Marostica, which boasts two ancient castles, one in the town and another on the hill above, and which just after the First World War found fame as the site of a living human chess game, still played on its main *piazza*. There were also R and R trips to Mestre, whose brothel, the Villa Rosa, Hemingway portrayed in fictional form in *A Farewell to Arms* – though according to his Red Cross colleagues in reality Hemingway resisted the charms of the girls and blushed when they accosted him.

What he really wanted to do was to get closer to the war. Before leaving for Italy he had thought of war as "something like a football game", according to his family, with America as the home team and the Austrians and Germans as the other side. The reality was rather different – and changed him for life.

2

Fossalta di Piave

"I'm going to see if I can't find out where the war is"
Hemingway to Ted Brumback, fellow Red Cross driver

PLEASANT AS LIFE in Schio might be, the war was very close – and the young Hemingway was impatient to take part in it. The Italians had occupied a trench line on the Asiago plateau and were holding it against the odds. In *A Farewell to Arms*, published a decade or so later, Hemingway gives a vivid description of the "flashes from artillery" lighting up the brown bare mountains beyond the crops and fruit trees.

The backdrop to the story is Gorizia, but the atmosphere it conveys is that experienced by the author in the Dolomites.

Sometimes in the dark we heard the troops marching under
the window and guns going past pulled by motor-tractors ...
To the north we could look across a valley and see a forest of
chestnut trees and behind it another mountain on this side of
the river. There was fighting for that mountain too. But it was
not successful, and in the fall when the rains came the leaves all
fell from the chestnut trees and the branches were bare and the
trunks black with rain.

With the rain came cholera, "but it was checked and in the end only seven thousand died of it in the army".

In Hemingway's much later novel *Across the River and Into the Trees* his alter ego Richard Cantwell recalls being an 18-year-old at the front in a cold winter, the mountains white beyond the plain, with the Austrians trying to break through

> where the Sile River and the old bed of the Piave were the only lines of defence. If you had the old bed of the Piave then you had the Sile to fall back on if the first line did not hold. Beyond the Sile there was nothing but bare-assed plain and a good road network into the Veneto plain and the plains of Lombardy, and the Austrians attacked again and again and again late through the winter to try to get onto this fine road they were rolling on now which led straight to Venice.

With the natural curiosity of a budding journalist fascinated by history, Hemingway now began to collect detailed information about Italy, Austria and the war which would later emerge in his fiction. He was gripped by the story of Cesare Battisti, a journalist who had been born in Trento – at the time part of Austro-Hungary – but had become an Italian patriot, fleeing to Italy in 1914 and joining the Alpini at the front to fight on Italy's behalf. Captured in 1916 during the battle for Monte Corno di Vallarsa (now Monte Corno Battisti) and taken back to Trento, Battisti was hung as a traitor. Hemingway kept a photo of him in his pocket, and also took his own photographs of the battlefront (now preserved at the Kennedy Library in Boston).

But other men's tales of war were not enough and despite his gruesome experiences at the munitions factory, Hemingway was still hungry for action. "I'm going to get out of this ambulance section and see if I can't find out where the war is", he told Theodore

(Ted) Brumback, a former colleague on the *Kansas City Star* and fellow Red Cross volunteer. The Americans of the 'Schio Country Club' drove their Fiat and Ford ambulances up the hairpin bends to Pasubio and back to evacuate the wounded: it was now that Hemingway first met Dos Passos, at least according to both writers' later accounts.

He asked to be moved to Section II of the American Red Cross at Roncade, but was itching to get even closer to the front, and volunteered to help Red Cross mobile canteens to deliver cigarettes, cigars and chocolates by bicycle to Italian Arditi special forces further up the frontline at Fossalta di Piave, some forty miles from Venice. The operation was based at Casa Botter, a three-storey whitewashed villa in its own grounds near the Piave River at Fornaci, a village within the environs of Monastier. The villa – though closed – still stands up a driveway on a straight country road lined with deep ditches, and still bears the coat of arms of the Botter family, a shield displaying an eagle with a lamb in its claws.

Hemingway felt lonely there. Other Red Cross drivers returned to Schio, but he stayed on, sometimes joining fellow American volunteers on the second floor of the Villa Albrizzi, a silk factory in San Pietro Novello near Monastier, a setting he would later use in 'Now I Lay Me', one of his short stories about the war. Though closed, unoccupied and somewhat dilapidated both Casa Botter and the Villa Albrizzi now display information boards proudly recording Hemingway's stays there. Also still standing, but partly converted into flats, is the nearby former Benedictine Abbey of Monastier, Santa Maria del Pero (meaning 'river port'), which served as a military hospital, its courtyard full of ambulances. The abbey's belfry served as a lookout tower and as a result was a favourite target for Austrian artillery.

Hemingway ate at the Italian army officers' mess of the 69th and 70th regiments of the Ancona Brigade, and here he met the army chaplain, Don Giuseppe Bianchi, from Florence, who was to play a key role in his later life and would feature in *A Farewell to Arms*. Another priest who played a prominent part in the war effort was Don Giovanni Minozzi, from Abruzzo, who with help from the YMCA had set up the soldiers' rest and recreation refuges ('Case del Soldato') in Veneto villas such as Casa Botter and Villa Albrizzi, with the aim of giving troops a respite from war which did not involve alcohol or brothels.

"I dispense chocolate and cigarettes to the wounded and the soldiers in the frontline", Hemingway wrote to a friend back in Chicago in June 1918. "Each aft and morning I load up a haversack and take my tin lid and gas mask and beat it up to the trenches." It was a brave gesture, but also foolhardy: the Austrians were mounting an onslaught across the Piave River. The conditions were appalling, the problem now being not ice and snow but mud, with the ground on either side of the river sodden after repeated rainstorms.

Hemingway was aware that a fellow American volunteer, Lieutenant Edward McKey, had been killed on a canal in the Piave area earlier in June during a previous Austrian onslaught known as the Battle of the Solstice, which lasted from 15 to 23 June. He even took a photograph of the spot where McKey had died. But he went ahead anyway. While helping to recover wounded Italian troops around midnight on 8 July – American Red Cross units from Roncade, Schio and Fanzolo rescued over 10,000 injured Italians during the battle – Hemingway was hit when Austrian troops on the other side of the river opened up with mortar and machine gun fire.

Wounded by shrapnel in both legs from a trench mortar bomb (*Minenwerfer*) which exploded next to him, Hemingway nonetheless somehow helped an Italian soldier who had been wounded in the chest to safety despite his own pain and shock. Limping from his own wounds, Hemingway hoisted the injured soldier on his shoulders and headed for his ambulance some distance away. He had only covered fifty yards when machine gun bullets tore into the knee of his already wounded right leg. He dragged himself and the soldier a further hundred yards before fainting.

A monument, erected in 1979, records the event: "On this embankment", the inscription reads, "Ernest Hemingway, a volunteer with the American Red Cross, was wounded on the night of 8 July 1918". Underneath is inscribed his remark "*Io sono un ragazzo del Basso Piave*" – "I am a boy of the Lower Piave". Beside it is a 1970s chapel dedicated to the "Ragazzi del '99", a reference to Italian youngsters who had been born in 1899 (as Hemingway himself was) and who were called up as teenagers to reinforce an increasingly desperate struggle to keep the Austrians at bay. A toll bridge crosses the Piave here, the successor to a bridge repeatedly blown up during the conflict. Spent cartridges and shells, even soldiers' remains, are still sometimes found in the area during building work.

What the memorial does not record is the searing impact of the explosion on Hemingway, a trauma which would remain with him forever. The actual spot where Hemingway was blown up was some 500 metres to the left of the monument, on a bend of the river where the Austrian troops were no more than sixty metres away on the other side. Standing there with Bruno Marcuzzo, a local military historian and Hemingway enthusiast, you can see clearly how close to danger Hemingway was. He had cycled there from the church of Pralungo, whose *campanile* you can still see across the fields from the nearby canals, which at the time were awash with bodies from both sides as the fighting raged back and forth across the frontier.

He left his bicycle at the house closest to the steep embankment and headed for the bunker cut into it, just below where the chapel now stands. Hemingway then made his way along the trench to a command post, and then down to the very edge of the river to a forward observation and listening post. He was not supposed to get so close to the frontline: very possibly he himself set off the Austrian barrage which followed, as Austrian watchers on the other side of the river heard suspicious movements and voices, and opened up.

In his story 'The Way You'll Never Be' Hemingway recalls the vivid image of the "yellow house" he saw to his left as the explosions shook the ground he was standing on. It was not in fact yellow, nor is it yellow now (for it is still there, used as a holiday let): the shutters are blue, and the walls are made of what the Italians call *cocciopesto*, or *opus signinum*, a building material first developed in ancient Rome and made of smashed-up tiles and pottery mixed with lime mortar and then pounded into a kind of plaster. To Hemingway, however, it may well have appeared yellow in the light of the flares the Austrians fired into the air to light up their targets.

Hemingway embellished and sometimes altered the story of his wounding in later years, and some biographers have cast doubt on his heroic actions, including reports that he had a silver plate put in his injured knee cap or that he was shot in the groin as well as the legs. The Red Cross report simply stated: "EM Hemingway was wounded by the explosion of a shell which landed about three feet from him, killing a soldier who stood between him and the point of explosion and wounding others."

However he was later awarded the Italian Silver Medal for Bravery and promoted to first lieutenant, and the citation reads: "Gravely wounded by numerous pieces of shrapnel from an enemy shell, with an admirable spirit of brotherhood, before taking care of himself, he rendered generous assistance to the Italian soldiers more seriously wounded by the same explosion and did not allow himself to be carried elsewhere until after they had been evacuated."

Ted Brumback wrote to Hemingway's parents that "an enormous trench mortar bomb" had exploded within a few feet of Ernest, and the concussion had knocked him unconscious and buried him in earth. The Italian standing between him and the explosion had been killed, another had had both legs blown off, and Ernest had carried a third badly wounded Italian on his back to the first-aid post. "He says he does not remember how he got there nor that he had carried a man until the next day when an Italian officer told him all about it ... Naturally, being an American, Ernest received the best of medical attention."

Ernest was being "showered with attention by American nurses", Brumback assured the family back in Chicago. "Wounded in legs by trench mortar; not serious; will receive valor medal; will walk in about ten days", Hemingway himself told them. He later described the experience to his friend and fellow journalist Guy Hickok, saying he had felt his soul coming out of his body "like you'd pull a silk handkerchief out of a pocket by one corner. It flew all around and then came back and went in again and I wasn't dead any more".

"The 227 wounds I got from the trench mortar didn't hurt a bit at the time, only my feet felt like I had rubber boots full of water on", Hemingway wrote shortly afterwards to his still anxious family in Chicago, adding "Hot water. And my knee cap was acting queer." The machine gun bullets which followed "just felt like a sharp smack on my leg with an icy snowball ... The Italian I had with me had bled all over my coat and my pants looked like somebody had made currant jelly in them and then punched holes to let the pulp out." The doctors "couldn't figure out how I had walked 150 yards with a load with both knees shot through and my right shoe punctured in two big places. Also over 200 flesh wounds."

"Got hit with a *Minenwerfer* that had been lobbed in by an Austrian trench mortar", Hemingway told his friend AE Hotchner many years later. "They would fill these *Minenwerfers* with the goddamnest collection of crap you ever saw – nuts, bolts, screws, nails, spikes, metal scrap – and when they blew you caught whatever you were in the way of ... They say I was hit with a machine gun afterward and that's when the kneecap went, but I think the *Minenwerfer* did the whole job."

The machine gun fire was not mentioned by Ted Brumback, nor for that matter in the Red Cross and Italian citations. Nonetheless, despite the fogs of war and memory, there is no doubt that Hemingway was badly wounded yet managed to help others. He was still only 18 years old. "When you go to war as a boy", he wrote later, "you have a great illusion of mortality. Other people get killed, not you. Then when you are badly wounded for the first time you lose that illusion, and you know it can happen to you."

In *A Farewell to Arms* Frederic Henry suffers a similar trauma: he is eating cheese and drinking wine at the frontline when he hears a "chuh-chuh-chuh-chuh" noise and sees a flash "as when a blast furnace door is swung open" with "a roar that started white and went red and on and on in a rushing wind". Unable to breathe, he thinks he is dead, but then hears screaming and the sound of machine gun fire. Frederic, who narrates the story, describes how he saw "the star shells go up and burst and float whitely and rocks going up and heard the bombs, all this in a moment, and then I heard close to me someone saying 'Mama Mia! Oh Mama Mia!'" His legs are "warm and wet": "I knew that I was hit and leaned over and put my hand on my knee. My knee wasn't there."

Hemingway was taken to a first-aid post in the mayor's house near the cemetery, and then carried three kilometres on a stretcher by Italian soldiers to a cowshed with no roof, the Casa Gorghetto, which has since been converted into a winery which offers 'Hemingwine' tours and bears a plaque in Italian, English and German recording that Hemingway "received his initial treatment in this house in the night on the 8th July 1918". Here he lay until five in the morning, his uniform soaked in blood. Hemingway said later he was surrounded by so many dead and dying men that death seemed a more natural state than life, and told a friend that as the delayed pain of his wounds hit him in the middle of the night he considered shooting himself with a pistol he had taken from the battlefield.

Instead he was taken for emergency treatment at a first-aid post housed in a primary school at Fornaci di Monastier (since demolished to make way for a housing estate), and given morphine and anti-tetanus injections. He was then treated for five days in a field hospital, Villa Toso, at Casier near Treviso, run by volunteers from the tiny republic of San Marino (now a private house), where doctors removed some of the shell fragments from his body and where he was almost certainly given penicillin against septicemia and gangrene, which killed many of those who had been badly wounded and often meant amputation for others who survived. "The doctors were working with their sleeves up to their shoulders and were red as butchers. There were not enough stretchers", he wrote later in *A Farewell to Arms*.

On 15 July 1918 he was transferred by train to the newly established American Red Cross hospital in Milan, where he arrived two days later, and where he was cared for by an attractive, tall, bubbly and dark-haired nurse from Washington, DC seven years his senior. Her name was Agnes von Kurowsky: the world knows her better as Catherine Barkley, the heroine of Hemingway's first bestseller.

3

Agnes and Catherine

"I always try to write on the principle of the iceberg. There is seven-eighths of it underwater for every part that shows"

Hemingway interviewed by George
Plimpton, *The Paris Review*, 1958

"**G**OD KNOWS I had not wanted to fall in love with her. I had not wanted to fall in love with any one. But God knows I had and I lay on the bed in the room of the hospital in Milan and all sorts of things went through my head but I felt wonderful..." So thinks Frederic Henry, Ernest Hemingway's alter ego in *A Farewell to Arms*, when Catherine Barkley comes to see him at the American hospital in Milan. "She looked fresh and young and very beautiful. I thought I had never seen anyone so beautiful."

Agnes von Kurowsky was 26, and Hemingway by now just 19. He was a patient at the newly opened Red Cross hospital at 4 Via Cesare Cantu, in the centre of Milan near the ornate Duomo. His letters home bear the letterhead "American Red Cross, La Croce Rossa Americana, Via Manzoni 10, Milano", leading biographers to suppose that Via Manzoni (closer to La Scala) was the scene of his romance with Agnes. But Via Manzoni was the Red Cross headquarters, where volunteers were given their training on arrival. A commemorative plaque at 6 Via Armorari, at right angles to Via Cesare Cantu and part of the same palazzo, records that this was the hospital where he recuperated, and where Agnes cared for injured soldiers as a wartime nurse.

Before the war it had been a small hotel or pensione: the Red Cross took over the third and fourth floors in June 1918. Hemingway recuperated in Room 106 on the fourth floor. The plaque on the building – today a bank – records Hemingway's stay there in the summer of 1918 "after being wounded at the Piave front", adding that this inspired the "true story" (*favola vera*) of *A Farewell to Arms*. On the back of one of his letters to his sister Marcelline in November 1918, Hemingway wrote – despite the Via Manzoni letterhead – that his actual address was the American Red Cross hospital at 4 Via Cesare Cantu. Marcelline had asked him whether a romance he had hinted at involved a Red Cross nurse. He replied that yes, it did, but he could not say more.

Henry Villard, a fellow ambulance driver and future US diplomat who was being treated for malaria and jaundice at Via Cesare Cantu in a room next to Hemingway on the fourth floor, later wrote that it was "a moderate-sized stone and stucco structure" which apart from the Red Cross emblem over the doorway had "nothing to indicate that it housed the first medical and surgical institution ever to be opened by Americans on Italian soil". In the half-light of the Milan street lamps, Villard said, it looked "as if it belonged to an era of horse carriages and opera lovers, of prosperous Lombardy bankers and businessmen".

It still had the pensione's furnishings, and the fourth floor, with its sixteen bedrooms, smelt of fresh paint and disinfectant. But it offered a view of red-tiled roofs and the "lofty spires" of the Duomo, with aircraft flying past from the landing strip in the suburb of Taliedo (one of the first airports in Italy, later abandoned) and now and then an airship, "a silver fish in an ocean of blue".

The hotel terrace, which ran round two sides of the building, had striped awnings, comfortable wicker armchairs, flower boxes and potted plants, and a table with magazines and a hand-cranked phonograph which played popular wartime songs such as 'Tipperary' and 'Keep the Home Fires Burning'. The third floor below housed the ten bedrooms of the nurses' quarters, as well as a dining room and a library that contained a piano and two singing canaries called George and Martha (after Washington and his wife), where patients gathered to socialise.

The patients also drank whatever alcohol they could find – brandy, vermouth, Cointreau – although not within sight or earshot of Katherine DeLong, the Canadian head nurse (the strict, even severe Miss Van Campen in the novel), who before the war had been nursing superintendent at the Bellevue Hospital in New York and was nicknamed 'Gumshoe', presumably because she moved quietly and kept an eye on things.

Villard (the "nice thin boy from New York with malaria and jaundice" in *A Farewell to Arms*) recalls being welcomed at the hospital by Agnes – a "tall, slender, chestnut-haired girl with friendly blue-gray eyes, who seemed to combine brisk competence with exceptional charm" – and being offered a "very dry Martini" as she put a thermometer in his mouth. The drink contained a medicinal "joker" in the form of a glob of castor oil instead of an olive, but was otherwise a "clear, cold American-style cocktail".

Hemingway always seemed to have a bottle of cognac "or some other spirituous liquor" hidden under his pillow. "'Here, have a swig!' he would say, wiping the neck of the bottle on a bedsheet." Known to all as 'Ernie', Hemingway was the life and soul of the party, Villard reports, a "big bear of a fellow" and a "good-looking son of a gun" with a strong jaw and a wide, boyish grin who authoritatively held court on matters from sport to the conduct of the war. He had a remarkable memory for detail: "Nothing escaped his interest: names, places, dates."

Hemingway underwent surgery for his injuries, with post-operative treatment and physiotherapy at the Ospedale Maggiore not far from the Porta Romana (now the Milan Polyclinic). He was soon able to get about on crutches. His was a "peach of a hospital", he wrote to his father, with "one of the best surgeons in Italy" attending to him. There was no lack of female attention either, since there were only four patients at first and eighteen Red Cross nurses to look after them. One of these, a brisk but motherly Scottish nurse called Elsie Macdonald, inevitably known to all as "Mac" ("plump and warm-natured", according to Villard) would become Catherine's friend Helen Ferguson in *A Farewell to Arms*. During the day, decorum – and Nurse DeLong – reigned. But then there were the nights – and Agnes was Hemingway's night nurse.

She was born in Pennsylvania: her father, Paul Moritz Julius von Kurowsky, was a naturalised American from a Polish-German family who taught languages in Washington, DC, where young Agnes became a librarian before training as a nurse at the Bellevue Hospital in New York as a more exciting alternative. She applied for Red Cross service in January 1918, and sailed for Europe from New York in June together with other Bellevue-trained nurses.

According to her passport details she was 5'8 and a brunette, with a mole on her right cheek. Agnes "had a sparkle the others didn't possess", Villard remembered, "fresh and pert and lovely in her long-skirted white uniform". She radiated "zest and energy". She was seldom to be seen in the daytime, but when she did appear "the entire place seemed to brighten because of her presence".

All the boys fell for Aggie, Villard recalled, but Hemingway was "smitten to a far greater extent" than the others. Villard was not aware at the time of the secret notes they exchanged, but "I knew that he had the inside track to her affections when I caught him holding her hand one afternoon in a manner that did not suggest she was taking his pulse". Agnes later maintained that Catherine Barkley, who in the novel is blonde, was based on her colleague Elsie Jessup, who had blue eyes and blonde hair, and who – like Agnes – was 5'8.

Elsie Jessup, a 31-year-old Red Cross nurse who had served previously with the Red Cross in Serbia – where she contracted typhus – worked alongside Agnes in Florence as well as Milan. Elsie had been engaged to an English officer killed in the war, and is sometimes said to have been English herself: in fact, although she had English mannerisms, at least according to Agnes (she carried a short cane, or swagger stick), Elsie was American. She was born in Pennsylvania, like Agnes herself, attended St Mary's School for Girls in Garden City in New York (later demolished) and trained as a nurse in New York, as Agnes had.

After six years overseas Elsie returned in April 1920 to her parents' home in Forest Hills, an affluent area of New York, with tales of the Bolsheviks torturing captured White Russian troops in Serbia "by burning holes in their arms and legs with hot irons", as the *Brooklyn Daily Eagle* reported at the time. Elsie was awarded the Serbian Cross of St Sava – the first woman to be given the honour – as well as several other medals for her service in Italy and the Balkans.

There is no doubt however that Hemingway chiefly had in mind Agnes herself: "Miss Barkley was quite tall. She wore what seemed to me a nurse's uniform, was blonde and had a tawny skin and gray eyes. I thought she was very beautiful." Frederic is instantly smitten, and steals her from under the nose of his roommate and rival, the Italian army doctor Lieutenant Rinaldo Rinaldi. The character of Rinaldi was based on Hemingway's real-life companion at the Milan hospital, Captain Enrico Serena, an Italian officer who wore a patch over one eye and courted Agnes by singing to her and kissing her hand (he was, Agnes noted in her diary at the time, "attractive in spite of his disfigurement").

In *A Farewell to Arms* Hemingway sets the Frederic-Catherine romance first at a British Red Cross hospital in the field: "At dinner

I ate very quickly and left for the villa where the British had their hospital. It was really very large and beautiful and there were fine trees in the grounds." According to the foremost Italian authority on Hemingway, the late Giovanni Cecchin, Hemingway almost certainly had in mind the three-storey, eighteenth-century aristocratic Villa Trento in Dolegnano del Collio, some ten miles from Gorizia in Friuli, just across the regional border from the Veneto.

The villa was the headquarters of a British ambulance unit which was headed by the historian George Macaulay Trevelyan and in which the future explorer and travel writer Freya Stark served as a VAD (Voluntary Aid Detachment) nurse. It had at various times hosted Italian royals, Napoleon and Pope Pius X before being turned over to the Red Cross in the First World War. Hemingway did not reach Friuli during the First World War – he only got to know it well much later, in the 1950s – but he would have known of the Villa Trento from British Red Cross colleagues at the front, and from accounts by Trevelyan himself.

In the novel Catherine too is a VAD nurse; she explains to Frederic that she is not strictly speaking a fully qualified nurse but a trained VAD volunteer, and is "on special behaviour" because "the Italians didn't want women so near the front". She slaps his face hard, a "sharp stinging flash", when he tries to kiss her ("I just couldn't stand the nurse's-evening-off aspect of it"), but succumbs when he apologises and then tries again: "I held her close against me and could feel her heart beating and her lips opened and her head went back against my hand and then she was crying on my shoulder. 'Oh darling' she said. 'You will be good to me, won't you?'"

Like Hemingway himself, Frederic is transferred to the newly installed American hospital in Milan, as is Catherine Barkley. Their love affair starts to intensify after he has recovered from his operation, when they can spend more time together enjoying Milan's cafes as well as midnight feasts back at the hospital with "anchovy sandwiches made of very tiny brown glazed rolls and only about as long as your finger ... Besides all the big times we had many small ways of making love."

4

Love at La Scala

"Milan is a peach of a town"

Hemingway to his mother Grace

WHETHER THE REAL AGNES and the real Ernest consummated their affair remains uncertain. Hemingway liked to give that impression: "It took a trained nurse to make love to a man with one leg in a splint", he told a friend. Much later in life he told AE Hotchner that when unable to sleep he focused on the events of his youth – trout fishing, camping in the woods, arguing with his mother, and "those nights when nurse Agnes von Kurowsky, who I stupidly hoped to marry, came to my bed in the hospital".

In a brief tale drawing on his hospital experiences called 'A Very Short Story', part of Hemingway's 1924 collection *In Our Time* and a sketch for *A Farewell to Arms*, the nurse is named Luz and the setting is moved to Padua. The narrator tells us that he "thought of Luz in his bed" when returning to the front after being nursed by her. He had even taken other patients' temperatures for Luz so that she would not have to leave his bed: "There were only a few patients, and they all knew about it."

The couple go to pray in the Duomo before he leaves for the frontline. "They wanted to get married, but there was not enough time for the banns, and neither of them had birth certificates." They agree to get married in the US when the war ends but quarrel when parting at Milan station because she is "not willing to come home at once" – a reflection of the real Agnes' reluctance to return to the US, as Hemingway later admitted to his fellow ambulance driver Bill Horne ("She doesn't want to come home at all").

Luz subsequently falls for a major in the Italian Arditi forces, writing to the narrator that "theirs had been only a boy and girl affair", though she "hoped he would have a great career, and believed in him absolutely". The Italian major however "did not marry her in the spring, or any other time", and the story ends with the narrator contracting gonorrhoea from a department store sales girl while riding in a taxi through Lincoln Park in Chicago.

Apart from the ending, this reflects Hemingway's experiences with Agnes – at least as he remembered them, or would have liked them to be. A 1997 film, *In Love and War*, directed by Richard Attenborough and starring Chris O'Donnell as Hemingway ('Ernie') and Sandra Bullock as Agnes, portrays the couple going to bed together at a rundown hotel which has become a brothel near the frontline, called – inevitably – the Pensione Rosa. Ernie is embarrassed at not finding a more suitable venue for their love making, but Agnes accepts the inevitable and undresses. "Oh Aggie, it wasn't supposed to be like this", the Hemingway character says. "We were going to be in the most beautiful place on God's earth." "Then close your eyes", Nurse Aggie whispers.

The film script takes other liberties too: the romance takes place not in Milan but at the field hospital at Bassano (where the film was shot) on the first floor above the Section I ambulance station. It is Agnes rather than the San Marino doctors who saves Ernie from having his leg amputated by administering antiseptic irrigation, presumably with sodium hypochlorite, to prevent gangrene, the method devised during the First World War by a British chemist, Henry Dakin, and a French surgeon, Alexis Carrel.

The Italian army doctor who wants to cut Ernie's leg off (and also to seduce Agnes) is Domenico Caracciolo, an aristocrat who in real life was indeed Hemingway's rival for Agnes' affections, but only much later, when Hemingway was already back in the US, and who was in any case not a doctor but an artillery officer. At the time when Hemingway was being nursed by Agnes the other contender for her hand was Captain Serena, who like Caracciolo was an army officer, not a surgeon. The film imagines a final meeting on Lake Walloon in Michigan, at which Agnes declares her love but Ernie says they have both changed. In reality they parted in Italy, and never met again.

The film does however effectively convey the brash young Hemingway's coming of age against the backdrop of war, and only claims to be "based on" a true story. The producer, Dimitri Villard, was the son of Henry Villard, Hemingway's fellow patient in Milan, who after Hemingway's death in 1961 was contacted for information by Carlos Baker, Hemingway's biographer. This led to Villard tracking down Agnes, who was by then living in Key West, Florida (though curiously she never met Hemingway there). When she died in 1984 at the age of 92, Villard obtained permission for Agnes to be buried at the US Soldiers' and Airmen's Home National Cemetery in Washington, DC, and her grateful husband, William Stanfield, gave her letters and diaries to Villard, who published them five years later in his book *Hemingway in Love and War* (written with James Nagel of the University of Georgia).

The letters date from periods when they were apart because either Hemingway or Agnes had left Milan for other parts of Italy. "Kid, my kid, I've just been in your room, and talk about chairs that whisper!" Agnes wrote to Hemingway on 25 September 1918, when he left for Stresa on Lake Maggiore. "That whole room haunted me so that I could not stay in it." And on 17 October, when she had been temporarily transferred to a hospital in Florence, she admitted to him that every girl likes to have some man tell her he can't do without her. "Anyway I am but human, and when you say these things I love it and can't help but believe you so don't be afraid I'll get tired of you. I haven't really started to worry yet over your forgetting to love me as you do now."

When he first gets to know Catherine in *A Farewell to Arms* Frederic dreams of taking her to the Cova cafe and bar (where later in the novel he buys her chocolates), and then "down the Via Manzoni in the hot evening" to a hotel where they would drink white wine from Capri (Capri Bianco, a blend of Falanghina and Greco) and make love naked with the windows open "and the swallows flying over the roofs".

Hemingway also implied in his letters that he and Agnes had made love, referring to her in a letter to a friend in America as his "Missus". Agnes herself later said however that she had not been "that kind of girl", and insisted it had all merely been "a flirtation". "Now Ernest Hemingway has a crush on me or thinks he has," she wrote in her diary on 25 August. Ernest was "far too fond of me and speaks in such a desperate way every time I am cool, that I dare not damper his ardor as long as he is here in the hospital. Poor kid, I am sorry for him."

There is some evidence that she fought off not only Hemingway but also the dashing Captain Serena, who while Hemingway was being operated on took her out to dinner at the Sempioncino restaurant, noted for its orchestra and dancing, on Corso Sempione, near the Sforza Castle (Castello Sforzesco). It turned out however that the captain had reserved a table in a private room with a couch in it. Agnes left early, saying she was on night duty and could not linger.

But Hemingway's passion was real enough: "I am in love again", Hemingway wrote to his parents back in Chicago. The feeling seemed to be mutual: "He was talking last night of what might be if he was 26–28", Agnes wrote in her diary in September. She wished in some ways that he was indeed her own age: "He is adorable, & we are congenial in every way."

She was alarmed when 'Mac' found one of her yellow hairpins under Hemingway's pillow. There were small intimacies: sitting on the balcony Agnes wiped his neck and chest with a moist towel when it was hot, and scratched the soles of his feet when they became itchy. He was "Ernie, my darling", "tesoro mia" (*tesoro* is a masculine noun in Italian, but the sentiment is clear). "I sometimes wish we could marry over here, but since that is so foolish I must try & not think of it", she told her diary on 1 December. In a wifely gesture at one point, albeit after "long persuasion", she washed his shirt for him – it was "getting a bit whiffy", he said – so he could go to the races properly dressed.

Although Red Cross nurses were barred from emotional involvement with patients, Agnes and Ernest exchanged love notes and even (despite 'Gumshoe') managed dinner dates at Biffi's, an elegant restaurant in the arcaded, glass-covered Galleria Vittorio Emmanuele near the Duomo. Famed for its risotto Milanese (and still today favoured by Milan's fashionable society), Biffi's was where Ernest and Agnes held hands and drank white wine with peaches in it.

No doubt they also frequented the Gran Italia, where in *A Farewell to Arms* Frederic and Catherine (against the advice of the head waiter) try sweet wines such as fresa (or freisa), deciding they prefer the dry whites of Capri after all. Milan, Hemingway wrote to his mother at the end of July 1918, was "the most modern and lively city in Europe". "We used to stop at Bellagio on Como for week ends from Milan during the war", he told the poet and editor Ernest Walsh in 1925, adding "but I don't remember names of pubs".

He enjoyed La Scala, which had been closed during the war but with the support of the Milan council (*comune*) now managed to stage some performances to support the war effort. Hemingway had seen Verdi's *Aida*, Renzo Bianchi's *Ghismonda*, two operas by Rossini, *Moses in Egypt* and *Barber of Seville*, and Arrigo Boito's *Mephistofele* (in which the 28-year-old Beniamino Gigli starred as Faust) – or so he told his music-loving, opera-trained mother, though he added that he would have preferred Bizet's *Carmen*, Puccini's *La Boheme* "or something interesting".

He also got to know "lots of the singers who hang around the American Bar". According to Agnes' diary, as well as attending the opening night of *Ghismonda* they saw a ballet, *Il Carillon Magico*, "the most delightful I've ever seen" – though the evening was somewhat spoiled when "Mr Hem got sick in the middle and had to leave". Hemingway also saw (or at least said he intended to see) Gabriele D'Annunzio's patriotic drama *La Nave* ('The Ship') set to music by the composer Italo Montemezzi.

Ernest and Agnes (again like Frederic and Catherine) even went to the San Siro race track together: the setting found its way into his story 'My Old Man', which is set in the racing world. "San Siro was the swellest course I'd ever seen", the narrator tells us: back in Milan he describes how he "went out of the Galleria and walked over to in front of the Scala and bought a paper".

Hemingway was especially fond of the elegant Cova bar and restaurant, at that time just round the corner from the La Scala opera house (it later moved to Via Montenapoleone), and famous for its rich pastries and panettone. The Cova, Hemingway wrote with obvious approval in his story 'In Another Country', was "rich and warm and not too brightly lighted, and noisy and smoky at certain hours, and there were always girls at the tables and the illustrated papers on a rack on the wall".

Hemingway was certainly attractive to women: he was admired as a wounded war hero by both women and men, and cut a romantic and stylish figure on crutches (later a cane) in his elegant officer's tunic and cape with a silver clasp, made for him by the Milan military tailor Fratelli Spagnolini (conveniently located next to Red Cross headquarters on Via Manzoni) and his leather cordovan boots. Agnes later said she would always remember the sight of him stepping out of the fourth floor lift at the hospital in his cape, holding out his arms to embrace her.

He was widely reported to be the first American to be wounded in Italy. This was not in fact the case, but the Chicago newspapers carried fulsome reports of his courage in carrying an Italian to safety despite his severe leg and knee injuries. His sister Marcelline later recalled that he had even featured in a newsreel shown in Chicago cinemas, sitting in a wheelchair on the hospital porch with a "pretty nurse", and their father had gone to see it repeatedly.

The "pretty nurse" may have been Agnes – but there is intriguing evidence that as he discovered the land of Italian opera, wine and beauty, young Ernest had other women in his sights as well.

5

The Torino Girl

"I almost married a girl here"

Hemingway to AE Hotchner

AT THE END of September 1918, two months after being injured, Hemingway obtained a ten-day convalescence pass and headed for Stresa on Lake Maggiore, staying – in typical Hemingway style – not at some modest pensione but at the Grand Hotel des Iles Borromees, where the room he occupied (106) is now The Hemingway Suite. He was waved off by Agnes – formally at first, Agnes wrote in her diary, since the stern Miss DeLong was "close at hand", but then "I slipped into the elevator with him & we had a more real farewell". She missed him terribly, she told her diary: there was a thunderstorm, "the mice ran back and forth", and it was "very dark and spooky ... the most dismal night I ever spent on night duty".

Hemingway by contrast was having a whale of a time. His companion at Stresa was a fellow injured Red Cross ambulance driver from Minnesota called Johnny Miller, attached to Section II of the ARC at Roncade. They played billiards with an elderly Italian aristocrat and former diplomat, Count Giuseppe Greppi (slightly altered to Count Greffi in *A Farewell to Arms*) who Hemingway boasted had "taken me under his wing". "Convalescing with some awfully nice Italian People", he wrote to his father on 26 September on a postcard from Mount Mottarone, with a view of the Italian-Swiss border.

The count, who claimed he was nearly 100 and had had affairs with "all the historical women of the last century", bought him champagne whether he won or lost at billiards, Hemingway said. He made boating trips to the island of Pescatori on the lake ("the most beautiful in Italy") and enjoyed dry martinis in the hotel bar. "I'm up here at Stresa, a little resort on Lake Maggiore", he wrote to his parents in distant Chicago, "One of the most beautiful Italian lakes". He had also learned "polite" Italian, he told his family (though in fact his Italian remained fairly patchy, with frequent mistakes).

At Stresa Hemingway also became acquainted with a family from Turin, Pier Vincenzo Bellia and his three daughters – Elda, 23, Dionisia, 20 and Bianca Maria, 17. Count Bellia, Hemingway wrote to his family back in Chicago, was "one of the richest men in Italy", and he and his wife "have adopted me and call themselves my Italian mother and father". Their three daughters were all "beautiful": Hemingway however seems to have fallen immediately in love with Bianca rather than her older sisters, and according to Giovanni Cecchin, who tracked down Bianca in Turin in 1981, over sixty years later, he even talked of marriage.

It came to nothing: her father ruled she was too young to get engaged, and Bianca agreed, telling Cecchin that although Hemingway had been undoubtedly handsome and likeable, "we knew almost nothing about him ... In any case I did not want to go and live in America". When Count Bellia visited Hemingway at the hospital in Milan, he took his middle daughter Dionisia with him rather than Bianca. Nonetheless the Bellias invited Hemingway to visit them in Turin, and he may have done so. "They have invited me to spend Christmas and my two weeks leave with them at Torino and I think I shall probably go", he wrote from Stresa on 29 September.

According to Johnny Miller, Pier Vincenzo Bellia, who Hemingway referred to as "My Italian Father", more closely resembled the cynical and worldly "Count Greffi" in *A Farewell to Arms* than Count Greppi did. Bianca agreed, "with the difference that my father was not an unbeliever, and the wine we drank was not champagne but Asti Spumante". "The Count Bellia wants me to spend a couple of weeks with them at Turino (sic)", Hemingway told his father in mid-November. "He has an awful lot of dough and is a peach of an old scout. The whole family are great and they treat me just like a son or like a prodigal son!"

Did he go? He had a rival invitation to go shooting in Abruzzo, and was dreaming of a trip to the south – Naples or Sicily. In the first half of December, as we shall see, he went to Treviso to see Agnes, and at the end of December he went to Taormina. Yet Hemingway once remarked to his friend AE Hotchner when they passed through Turin in 1954 while en route to Cuneo that he had "almost married a girl here".

According to Hotchner in his memoir *Papa Hemingway*, Hemingway then added "Red Cross Nurse. I was laid up here in the base hospital because of the leg." Asked by Hotchner if "the Torino girl you nearly married" went into *A Farewell to Arms*, Hemingway replied "Sure. Everything that happened to me in Italy went into it, one way or another. The Torino girl was Catherine Barkley, and so were some others ... The way Lieutenant Henry felt when Catherine Barkley let down her hair and slipped into his hospital bed was invented from that girl in Torino – not copied, *invented*. The real Torino girl was a Red Cross nurse. She was beautiful and we had a wonderful love affair while I was hospitalized during the summer and fall of 1918."

What had happened between them, Hemingway said, was "pretty much as I wrote in 'A Very Short Story'". Unlike Catherine the Turin nurse had not become pregnant, let alone had a Caesarean: those details in *A Farewell to Arms* had come from the pregnancy of his second wife Pauline. But the Turin Red Cross nurse was "most of Catherine, plus some things that were of no woman I had ever known".

At first sight Hemingway, who in 1954 was recovering from plane crash injuries and suffering from both ill health and excessive drinking, seems to be confusing Turin with Milan: 'A Very Short Story' undoubtedly reflects his relationship with Agnes. In the original version the nurse was called 'Ag' rather than 'Luz': he only changed the name to Luz, Hemingway told his editor Maxwell Perkins, because Ag was "short for Agnes" and therefore "libellous".

But did he in fact have an affair in Turin as well as in Milan? On 14 November he wrote to his father that his "Italian father", Count Bellia, had sent him a "wonderful big box of chocolates", adding that "he and the family are very good to me". The next known letter is nine days later, to his sister Marcelline – though in that letter Hemingway tells her he is in love with Ag and she with him, adding "I'm not foolish and think I can get married now but when I do marry I know who I'm going to marry and if the family don't like it they can lump it and I never will come home".

In a letter to his family on 28 November, Thanksgiving Day, Hemingway outlined all the invitations he had received to "various parts of Italy", adding, again, "The Bellias want me to stay a couple of weeks at Turino". Cecchin concluded that Hemingway may indeed have visited the Bellias, and had perhaps been laid up in a Turin hospital with a relapse of his injuries or an after-effect of surgery sometime in November or December 1918.

In January 1978 the Italian author and film director Mario Soldati, who had published an article on the mystery of Hemingway's 'Torino girl', received a letter from a former head nurse at the Mauriziano Umberto I hospital in Turin, which is still on Corso Filippo Turati (formerly Corso Stupinigi), between the Olympic Stadium and the

Egyptian Museum, although the original nineteenth-century building was badly bombed during the Second World War.

The head nurse, who was by this time elderly, unwell and wished to remain anonymous, told Soldati that she had been at the Mauriziano hospital in 1918 when one of her nurses, a blonde girl called Maria, had become pregnant by an American writer called "Ernesto", who had been admitted to the Turin hospital with bronchial pneumonia and had written Maria love poems. The pregnancy had caused difficulties for Maria with her family, but she went ahead with it, and the resulting baby boy had become a local lawyer who bore "an extraordinary resemblance to Ernest Hemingway".

All efforts by Soldati and Cecchin to establish the truth of this assertion met with a discreet silence: Soldati tried to follow the claim up but the elderly head nurse – who said in her letter to him that she had photographs of both the nurse and her little boy – did not reply. Soldati had at first thought that her letter was perhaps a hoax, but became convinced that it was genuine. On the other hand, according to the Italian historian Sergio Perosa, when Hemingway took his first wife Hadley to see "his" Italy in 1922, he included Turin in their itinerary and took her to meet the Bellia family, which he would seem unlikely to have done if he had a guilty secret to hide.

A further complication is that Hemingway appears to have had yet another girlfriend known to his fellow volunteers as 'La Turini', though in Milan rather than Turin. One of Hemingway's pals in Milan, a First Lieutenant in the 332nd Infantry Regiment from Philadelphia called Carl Hugo Trik, had acquired an Italian girlfriend called Pia; he and Hemingway went to a dance at the Cova on Christmas Day 1918, he told Carlos Baker. Hemingway's date for the evening was a pretty, dark-haired nurse who "stood on a chair and made an impassioned speech about cabbages and kings" (from 'The Walrus and the Carpenter' in Lewis Carroll's *Alice in Wonderland*) and played charades in Italian with them.

In his account of Hemingway and Dos Passos at the Italian front, Cecchin identifies this playful nurse as "Miss Turini", who, however, was not the mystery nurse from Turin but rather Mercedes Turrini, a vivacious, smiling, dark-haired Italian auxiliary nurse listed in Charles Bakewell's *The Story of the American Red Cross in Italy* (1920) as an Italian "nurses' aid" in Milan, and who appears in a photograph of Red Cross nurses in Milan together with the rather more motherly figures of Elsie MacDonald, Agnes Conway and Loretta Cavanaugh. Her youth, dark looks and bright smile do indeed make her the most likely candidate. Possibly Mercedes and Maria the Turin nurse were as much Luz in 'A Very Short Story' as Agnes was. Luz after all is a veiled reference to the Virgin Mary (Maria), or in Spanish Nuestra Senora de la Luz, 'The Lady of Light', and so for that matter is Mercedes – Maria de las Mercedes, or 'Mary of Mercies'.

Hemingway, in other words, fell for at least four young women in Italy while still in his late teens, and seems to have contemplated marriage to most if not all of them. He had form in this respect. While in New York en route to Italy he told his sister Marcelline and a number of chums that he had met and fallen in love with the silent film actress Mae Marsh, star of DW Griffiths' 1915 epic *The Birth of a Nation* (which he had seen with his grandfather Anson), and that they were engaged to be married. This was a complete invention, but deeply alarmed Hemingway's parents. When Hemingway finally admitted it was untrue his father wrote to him in fury, saying the "joke" had cost them sleepless nights.

6

Bassano del Grappa

"We were billeted in an old villa in Bassano ..."
Hemingway, 'The Passing of Pickles McCarty'

EVEN IF THE YOUNG Hemingway had other flirtations, there is no doubt that Agnes was the girl who truly captured his heart. There were, however, signs from the start that the romance would not last. She and Hemingway continued to write effusive letters to each other when she was transferred by the Red Cross first to Florence, working at the American Red Cross hospital for wounded Italians on Via di Camerata (still today an Italian Red Cross clinic), and then to a US field hospital near Treviso. He was, she wrote, the light of her existence, her hero. But they spent longer periods apart as the war neared its end and both Ernest and Agnes were assigned to frontline duties again.

Having recuperated from his operation Hemingway returned to duty on 18 October, heading first to Schio but then to the historic town of Bassano del Grappa in the foothills of the Dolomites, where Section I of the American Red Cross ambulance units was housed in the fifteenth-century Ca' Erizzo, alongside the Brenta River. Part of the Republic of Venice in the fifteenth century, the town was originally known as Bassano Veneto: the name was changed after the First World War in honour of the battles on Mount Grappa above rather than after the drink, though locals are also justifiably fond – and proud – of grappa, which is made from the pressings of discarded grape seeds and stalks (known as pomace).

Despite its batterings during both world wars – the price of its strategic location in the foothills of the Dolomites – Bassano today is much as it was, a charming walled town whose ultra-modern civic museum features a reminder of past glories in the works of a celebrated local painter, the sixteenth-century artist Jacopo Bassano. The Brenta once provided a vital trade and communication link with Venice; the famous covered wooden bridge over the Brenta River, originally designed by Palladio, was repeatedly destroyed by war but restored after the Second World War by the Alpini.

The long three-storey Ca' Erizzo Luca stretches along the Brenta riverbank on what is now Lungobrenta Hemingway, and a church with a striking hexagonal tower stands to the left of the entrance gates to the park behind the villa. From the old town above the villa you can see Mount Grappa and the Dolomites looming just beyond – the frontline in 1918 as the four-year war neared its end.

Renato Luca, the present owner and a keen hunter, opened a Wildlife Museum in the villa in the 1990s. The main attraction now however is the fascinating museum (open to the public at weekends and during the week by arrangement) devoted to Hemingway and the First World War. Inspired in part by the researches of the late historian Giovanni Cecchini, and run by a team headed by Luca's son Alberto, it offers meticulously researched photographs and documents, a collection of first editions of Hemingway in English and Italian and even a tableau of the writer at his desk with a zebra skin spread on the floor and a stuffed lion and cheetah by his side.

"We were billeted in an old villa in Bassano on the Brenta, on the east bank of the river, up beyond the covered bridge", Hemingway wrote in his story 'The Passing of Pickles McCarty'. "Big marble thing it was, cypress trees as you come up the drive, statues on either side and all the trimmings. We were the usual flat-footed, cock-eyed bunch of adventurers who couldn't make the army and had taken the ambulance."

From Bassano he watched a massive Italian artillery barrage which lasted all night and lit up the mountains above them. It was the start of what would become the Vittorio Veneto offensive against the Austrian forces, the beginning of the end. Hemingway later gave the impression that he had himself taken part in the attacks on Mount Grappa together with the special forces IX assault unit, the Arditi (the Daring), which was based at Bassano at the time.

He certainly later informed the Oak Park Memorial Committee that he had "participated" in the Mount Grappa offensive when it asked returning war veterans to "fill out a data sheet" so that the records of their war service would be "accurate and complete". This is widely regarded as another of his empty boasts – though some Italian historians, such as Cecchini, believe it is possible that he did get somewhere near the battlefront. What is undoubtedly true is that he contracted jaundice, and after just a week at Bassano went back to Milan to be treated.

He had a brief reunion with Agnes at the US field hospital at Dosson near Treviso, the Villa De Reali, named after the De Reali family which built the villa and extensive park in the nineteenth century on the site of a Benedictine abbey (it is now owned by the Canossa family, and used for conferences and weddings as well as cultural and garden events). Hemingway made the 200-mile trip there in early December 1918 in a convoy of army trucks and staff cars via Padua, Verona and Torreglia, where he was "treated royally" by British officers of the Royal Garrison Artillery, even taking part in a hunt on horseback.

The Villa De Reali at Dosson was the base of the 332nd Ohio Regiment. The base hospital's main job at this stage was not to deal with war wounds so much as to treat outbreaks of the equally dangerous 'Spanish flu', the 1918 epidemic which killed more people than the war itself. At Dosson those who died of it were accompanied to the local cemetery by a military band playing funeral marches on the way there but Dixieland tunes on the way back, stopping at an inn for wine and chestnuts, presumably to celebrate survival.

This may explain why Hemingway told a friend in marine aviation, Bill Smith, that Agnes had on this occasion refrained from "lecturing" him about alcohol, saying "Kid we're going to be partners. So if you are going to drink I am too. Just the same amount." "Bill this is some girl", Hemingway wrote. Together they made the first of several return visits Hemingway would make throughout his life to Fossalta di Piave and the riverbank where he had been wounded.

It was to be their last meeting however, and although they did not know it – or at least, Hemingway did not – their farewell at the villa gates was final. Agnes had told her diary when Hemingway returned from the Stresa trip that it was "wonderful to be together again", and while she was in Florence they exchanged numerous letters. In September she had even given 'the Kid' a ring: she told him she dreamed of him, and signed herself in at least one Florence letter as 'Mrs Kid'. Miss Jessup considered that he was just an "infatuated youth", Agnes said, but she knew he loved her, and sometimes wanted to "blurt it all out". "I love you Ernie", she declared at one point when she was in Florence. "In spite of the sunshine, I am lost without you. I thought it was the dismal rain that made me miss you so."

Hemingway and Agnes exchanged love letters for a while after the war ended and Hemingway returned to the United States. But in March 1919 Agnes wrote to Hemingway that she had met and fallen in love with Domenico Caracciolo. She was still "very fond" of "the Kid", but "more as a mother than a sweetheart".

In reality she had liked rather than loved Hemingway, Agnes

told Henry Villard many years later, finding him an impulsive and impetuous young man who "didn't really know what he wanted". Caracciolo, by contrast, she judged to be "completely sincere" as well as irresistibly attractive. Agnes was later rejected however as a suitable wife for Domenico by the Caracciolo family, above all his mother, who saw Agnes as an "American adventuress".

She tried to keep on good terms with Hemingway by letter, writing to him in 1922 to say how proud she would be some day to say, "Oh, yes, Ernest Hemingway. Used to know him quite well during the war." She continued to serve in the Red Cross in Romania and Haiti, and went on to marry twice. She and Hemingway never met again. But at the time Hemingway, who had "forgotten all about religion and everything else because I had Ag to worship", was "smashed" by her rejection of him, taking to his bed in his parents' home at Oak Park in a fit of despair. "She doesn't love me Bill", he wrote to his friend Bill Horne at the end of March 1919. "She takes it all back". He had hoped to marry her, and still loved her "so damned much", but "now the bottom has dropped out of the whole world".

Agnes had been Hemingway's first love, and her decision to break with him evidently lay behind his life-long preoccupation in his novels with romances which end in loss or failure. It may also have influenced his tendency in real life to break off a relationship before the woman could do so. After being "gypped" by Agnes, he wrote to Howell Jenkins, a former fellow Red Cross volunteer, in June 1919, he had "set out to cauterize out her memory and I burnt it out with a course of booze and other women and now it's gone".

His attitude to women was a mixture of tenderness and violence. According to the distinguished journalist Martha Gellhorn, his third wife, "Ernest had a theory that brutality was all women understood" – though in her profile of him for the *New Yorker* Lilian Ross, who got to know Hemingway well in the 1950s, found him "generous" and "warm-hearted".

Hemingway would return to his traumatic teenage wartime experiences throughout his life. It was now that he began to think more deeply about love – and death. "Dying is a very simple thing", he wrote to his family in October 1918. "I've looked at death, and really I know". How much better to die in youth and "go out in a blaze of light", he thought, than to die in old age when your body was worn out and your illusions had all been shattered.

But at the end of 1918 he still had a life ahead of him, and after a series of post-Armistice parties in Milan he was ready to return to America – though not before an interlude in another enchanting part of Italy, this time far from the mountains of the northeast: the island of Sicily.

7

Taormina

"I'm so homesick for Italy that when I write about it it has that
something about it that you only get in a love letter"

Hemingway to James Gamble, 3 March 1919

HEMINGWAY ONCE CLAIMED that when he travelled to
Taormina after his experiences on the Italian front and his
recuperation in the Milan hospital, he spent the entire week in bed
with a beautiful Sicilian woman.

He had seen nothing of the island except the view from his
bedroom window, he told his friend Eric Dorman-Smith (later Dor-
man-O'Gowan), an Irish-born British officer known as 'Chink' who
had fought on the Italian front and had got to know Hemingway at
the Anglo-American club in Milan, close to La Scala. The reason he
had only seen the view from his bedroom, Hemingway told Chink,
was that the landlady in the first small hotel he stayed in had hidden
his clothes and "kept him to herself" for a week.

The claim reflects Hemingway's love of exaggeration and tall
stories, but it also reflects his tendency to confuse his life and his
fiction to the extent that he himself probably did not know the
difference. Sometimes he blamed his publishers, telling his friend
Bill Smith in July 1927 that the "blurb and publicity writers" had

dreamed up the myth that he had been a bullfighter while serving in the French and Italian armies. The "invented and legendary crap" was "formidable", he said, adding "I have made it a point not to ever furnish a paragraph of biographical material".

Hemingway was however not beyond inventing the biographical myths himself: he once told Sylvia Beach, owner of the Paris bookshop Shakespeare and Company, that he had left home at the age of 14 rather than 18. During and even after the war he wore an Italian army uniform to which he was not entitled, though some Italian scholars suggest he may indeed at some point have "crossed the line" and taken part in some form of military action at the front instead of just distributing food and cigarettes.

But he did not – as he told his father – "hold rank" in both the American Red Cross and the Italian army: a photograph of him on a bicycle in front of the destroyed church at Fossalta di Piave, before he was wounded, shows him wearing what appears to be an Italian army uniform and carrying a rifle and grenades. Hemingway had left the Red Cross to "get a little action" and had held the rank of second lieutenant "in the Italian army", he misinformed a friend back home shortly before he was wounded.

He sometimes claimed not only that he had "fought" with the Arditi at the Piave front, when he had only served in a support role, but also that he had fought in campaigns which in reality occurred after he had been hospitalised. "Born in Oak Park, Illinois, served in war on Italian front, wounded, profession newspaper correspondent" were the opening lines of the potted autobiography he sent to the magazine editor Ernest Walsh in January 1925, neglecting to add that his war service on the Italian front had involved ambulances and mobile canteens.

Henry Villard later recalled that for many years the "publisher's blurb" on Hemingway's book covers stated – quite wrongly – that he had "served as an ambulance driver and infantryman with the

Italian army". Much later, during the Second World War, he implied that he had landed with US troops on D-Day (which he had not), writing to his son Patrick in September 1944 that "it has been about 2 months since Papa came back to France after landing on D Day on Omaha beach".

Hemingway was well aware of his tendency to exaggerate, and rather disarmingly even made fun of it in his story 'Soldier's Home', in which Harold Krebs, a Methodist from Kansas and a former Marine, comes back from the First World War in 1919 only to find that people at home are already weary of returning soldiers' tales. As a result he starts to lie in order to be "listened to at all": "His lies were quite unimportant lies and consisted in attributing to himself things other men had seen, done or heard of, and stating as facts certain apocryphal incidents familiar to all soldiers." When the first film version of *A Farewell to Arms* came out in 1932, Hemingway issued a statement disclaiming "the romantic and false military and personal career imputed to him" in the publicity material. He had only driven an ambulance "and was never involved in heroic actions of any sort".

So while in Taormina Hemingway did not, as far as we know, spend an entire week in bed with a woman – but he did conceive a story about an American soldier's affair with a Sicilian woman with "eyes like inkwells" and "full red lips". Called 'The Mercenaries', the idea for the story came to Hemingway while he was staying near Mount Etna overlooking the Bay of Naxos, where he enjoyed the bougainvillea, the lemon and orange groves, the sea changing from sky blue in the morning to purple in the evening and Sicilian wine, which had "the fire of the volcano and the sun of Sicily in it".

It must have been a welcome change from war-weary Milan. With the war now officially over Captain James Gamble, the officer who had been in charge of the mobile canteens at the front and therefore Hemingway's superior officer, had rented "a little house and garden belonging to an English artist" for a few months at Taormina, or so he wrote to Hemingway. An amateur painter, Gamble had accompanied Hemingway on the train to Milan after he was wounded, and visited him often in hospital. The only thing lacking in Taormina was company, he wrote, "and I only hope you will take care of that. There is plenty of room in the house, two studios, lots of atmosphere, and I should think plenty about which to write."

In fact according to the late Sicilian writer Gaetano Saglimbeni, who reconstructed the Taormina episode, Hemingway, Gamble and Colonel Tom Bartley, another American who had served at the front, were the guests of the 65-year-old Duke of Bronte, Alexander Nelson-Hood, great grandson of Admiral Nelson. Alexander – known as Alec – had been Duke since 1904: this was Italian high society, and quite a contrast with dark, cold, wartime Milan.

Although he was never to go there, Nelson had been rewarded with the estate at Maniace, a former Benedictine abbey, on the slopes of Mount Etna, and the title of Duke of Bronte by a grateful Ferdinand of Bourbon, King of the Two Sicilies. Nelson had rescued Ferdinand, his wife Maria Carolina and their entourage in Naples during the French-backed uprising of January 1799 by taking them to Palermo aboard his flagship, HMS *Vanguard*.

The rebellion was short-lived. In June the King was able to return to Naples under British protection and thousands of the rebels were executed – including Ferdinando Caracciolo, former head of the rebel naval forces (and a forebear of the Domenico Caracciolo who over a century later was to play a role in the Hemingway story by capturing the heart of Agnes von Kurowsky).

On Nelson's death the Bronte estate passed not to Horatia, his daughter by Emma Hamilton, but to his brother William. It then passed to Charlotte, William's daughter, and her husband Samuel Hood, Viscount Bridport; to their son Alexander Nelson-Hood; and then to his son of the same name, the fifth Duke of Bronte, who by the time of Hemingway's visit was the author of a book entitled

Sicilian Studies and a noted literary host and man of letters. Known as Castello Nelson, it is now a tourist attraction an hour's drive from Taormina.

Hemingway however almost certainly stayed – or at least, spent much of his time – not on the Bronte estate but at the equally luxurious clifftop villa owned by the Dukes of Bronte at Taormina itself, the eighteenth-century Villa La Falconara, with a ten-acre garden overlooking the stunning Bay of Naxos. Possibly the house with two studios mentioned by Gamble was in the extensive grounds, or nearby: Gamble's reference to an "English artist" may have been to the artist Robert Hawthorn Kitson, whose visitors at the celebrated Casa Cuseni (later restored by Kitson's niece Daphne Phelps and now an upmarket B&B) included DH Lawrence and Bertrand Russell.

Jim Gamble was not, as some Hemingway biographers have supposed, a wealthy member of the Cincinatti Procter and Gamble soap dynasty. As Gerry Brenner pointed out in *The Hemingway Review* in 2000, he was from Pennsylvania, not Cincinatti, and his family had made its money in the timber business. He was, however, a well-off Yale graduate in his mid-thirties, and as the officer in charge of the operation supplying Italian troops at the Piave front with chocolate and cigarettes he became so fond of young Hemingway that he apparently offered to pay for him to remain in Italy, all expenses paid, and to go with him to Madeira, gestures which Hemingway refused. Agnes for one strongly advised him against it, later explaining that Hemingway was "very fascinating to older men".

This has given rise to speculation that Gamble was sexually attracted to Hemingway: there is no evidence that he was gay (he married in 1926), but there is no doubt that Taormina (like Capri) was something of a homosexual expatriate Anglo-American colony at the time, and that many of its aristocratic and artistic community (including Kitson) were gay.

Hemingway later distanced himself from Gamble, but they nonetheless remained friends. "Every minute of every day I kick myself for not being at Taormina with you", Hemingway wrote to Gamble in March 1919 when he was back in Oak Park. "It makes me so damned homesick for Italy and whenever I think that I might be there and with you." He still remembered strolling with Gamble through old Taormina by moonlight, with "the moon path on the sea and Aetna fuming away and the black shadows and the moonlight cutting down the stairway back of the villa".

The fifth duke was a social celebrity with Royal connections (he had been gentleman usher to Queen Victoria and private secretary to her daughter) and held not just conservative but far-right views (he later supported Mussolini and Fascism). But he saw Italy, in Lucy Riall's words, as a place of "warmth, beauty and imagination" to which Northerners could escape and indulge their "secret desires". He also improved agriculture, irrigation, orange groves and wine making on the Bronte estate.

Hemingway found the duke to be a "charming and generous" host who enjoyed the company of writers, from TS Eliot, Somerset Maugham and Gabriele d'Annunzio to DH Lawrence – although Lawrence (who visited Bronte not long after Hemingway, in 1920, while living in the Villa Fontana Vecchia at Taormina) was less than complimentary, writing to Lady Cynthia Asquith that the estate was a "rather wonderful place" but adding "Mais mon Dieu, M. le Duc...", and describing the duke to another correspondent as "gaga".

Hemingway by contrast enjoyed the company of the duke and the table talk of his fellow Americans during his stay, not to mention the "robust and fragrant" Sicilian wine and the "strong flavours" of local cuisine. Years later, in 1950, he told General Charles 'Buck' Langham that when he was 19 years old two men aged over 90, Count Greppi at Stresa and "the Duke of Bronte who was a descendant of Nelson", had tried to "bring me up so I would have the beautiful manners a

Gentleman should have". "My salutations to the Duke of Bronte", he wrote to Jim Gamble a few months after the Taormina episode, in March 1919, when he was back in the United States.

He took long walks in the mornings down "picturesque lanes, between old houses with stone walls semi-covered by bougainvillea", avenues that opened onto lemon and orange groves and hills covered by the dark green of the olive trees. At night he could admire the light of the moon over Mount Etna.

And he started writing again. Set in Taormina, the story of 'The Mercenaries' is told in a bar in Chicago by Perry Graves, an American soldier-turned-mercenary. Perry tells his audience that he was once challenged to a duel while enjoying a candlelit dinner with a bewitching Sicilian lady he met by chance on the train from Rome to Taormina. The train took them past the scenery of lemon and orange groves, "so pretty that it hurts to look at it", and through the terraced hills of olive trees, yellow fruit and streams "with wide dry pebbly beds cutting down to the sea and old stone houses".

After dinner – antipasto, soup, flat fish, roast young turkey "with a funny dressing" and pasticceria, all washed down by "Bronte wine that's like melted up rubies" – he and the lady repaired to the garden of the hotel under the orange trees, "jasmine matted on the walls, and the moon making all the shadows blue-black and her hair dusky and her lips red". After admiring the moon on the water and the snow on Mount Etna they went to bed together – or so Perry implies. The lady was married to an Italian pilot, but "it seemed she and her husband didn't get along so well... she was pleased and happy that I had come to cheer her up for a few days. And I was too."

But at breakfast the next day ("or what they call breakfast, rolls, coffee and oranges") who should appear but the husband, an Italian Air Force ace of "irresistible charm" but also "callous and brazen", nicknamed Il Lupo (The Wolf). This character calls to mind Gabriele D'Annunzio – though Hemingway was almost certainly thinking of another well-known daredevil pilot, Fulco Ruffo di Calabria. Il Lupo, whose face is familiar to Perry from illustrated magazines, is "a good-looking fellow with a scar across his cheek and a beautiful blue theatrical-looking cape and shining black boots and a sword". He goes white when he sees his wife with her lover, demanding "Who are you, son of a dog?"

Il Lupo challenges Perry to a duel, and since the American does not have a sword they settle for handguns. The two men are supposed to fire their pistols in the restaurant garden on a count of three given by the waiter, but the Italian cheats by trying to fire before three is reached, and Graves shoots the pistol out of his hand. He then leaves, calmly drinking his by now cold cup of coffee before leaving. The lady puts her arms round Il Lupo, whose face is red with shame and whose hand is wounded, and her eyes flicker at the departing Perry over her injured husband's shoulder. "Maybe it was a wink, maybe not."

Before long Hemingway, back in the United States, was telling the story to friends in Petoskey – with himself in the role of the courageous mercenary challenged to a duel over a beautiful woman, although in this version he was able to escape because his mistress distracted his rival. The fantasy, Hemingway's biographer Michael Reynolds has suggested, carries echoes of D'Annunzio, who was himself given to flights of fancy and had fictionalised his affair with the actress Eleanora Duse in his novel *Il Fuoco* (*The Flame*), copies of which (in translation) Hemingway gave to several of the women he pursued after the war.

Much later, and after another world war, Hemingway would write *Across the River and Into the Trees*, about the love of the ageing American Colonel Cantwell for Renata, a young and beautiful Italian girl. "On the Venetian canals where D'Annunzio's poet and actress played out their romantic tryst in *The Flame*", Reynolds comments, "Cantwell and Renata romance in a gondola ... The fantasies of young men are difficult to keep down; from the bubbling pot they rise up in various guises."

Hemingway did not tell Agnes about his Taormina adventure. He sent 'The Mercenaries' to *Red Book* magazine, but it was rejected because it lacked female reader appeal or "heart interest", or so Hemingway claimed. It was only published in 1985, in *The New York Times Magazine*, after it had been found by Peter Griffin, a Hemingway biographer, among documents donated by Mary Hemingway, the writer's fourth and last wife, to the US National Archives in Boston.

8

In Another Country

"God bless my brother gone to war"
American eighteenth-century bedtime prayer

DESPITE THE LURE of exotic Sicily, Hemingway remained attached to both the Veneto and Milan as he prepared to return to the US. "The memory of the north of Italy in 1918 would stay with him all the rest of his life", as his biographer Carlos Baker observed. The memory of his wartime experiences in northern Italy produced enduring works of fiction, above all *A Farewell to Arms*, the title taken from a sonnet by the sixteenth-century dramatist George Peele. If the story has a sad ending, this reflects Hemingway's disappointment over Agnes' rejection of him rather than disillusionment with Italy as such.

Part of the power of *A Farewell to Arms*, as James Nagel has pointed out, derives from the fact that it reflects not Hemingway's optimistic mood when he left Italy in 1918 "after the victorious conclusion of the war with the expectation of a life with Agnes", but rather his subsequent, darker experiences – the loss of Agnes, the suicide of his father, his two marriages and the near death of his second wife Pauline in childbirth. The novel's hero, Frederic Henry, is older than Hemingway was, arrives in Italy much earlier and therefore lives through the disaster of Caporetto rather than the triumph of Vittorio Veneto.

Frederic is taken for a deserter during the rout which follows the battle of Caporetto, and jumps into the Tagliamento River in Friuli to escape the firing squad. He is eventually re-united with the by now pregnant Catherine, but when they escape to Switzerland she dies in childbirth. Hemingway's description of the Caporetto disaster was so vivid that many readers thought he must have witnessed it, when in fact the rout had occurred before he even set sail for Europe and the battlefront. He had however absorbed tales of Caporetto from the soldiers he spent time with in 1918 at Monastier and Fossalta, for whom it would still have been a recent – and traumatic – memory.

The biographer Michael Reynolds has suggested that Hemingway drew on the First World War articles and diaries of the Italo-American journalist Gino Speranza. He was also most probably familiar with the work of the historian GM Trevelyan, who was head of the First Ambulance Unit of the British Red Cross. Forced to evacuate the Villa Trento field hospital in Friuli after Caporetto, Trevelyan retrenched at Schio. There he wrote a detailed account of his experiences at the front in the run up to the retreat which was published in June 1918 in the *Anglo-Italian Review*, and which Hemingway must have seen either at Schio itself or later at the Anglo-American club in Milan, close to the hospital where he was treated.

After Caporetto, Trevelyan led relief operations both in the Piave basin and on the 7000-feet Pasubio massif above. In 1919 he published a book-length version of his reminiscences, *Scenes From Italy's War*, praising Hemingway's hero Cesare Battisti, whose "soul seemed to haunt the rocks of Pasubio, pointing down towards Trento, where they hanged him for a traitor". With the war over, however, the Austro-Hungarian rulers had been "justly paid", "trampled out of sight" by their subjects in the "ramshackled empire" they had filled with blood, wailing and oppression for too long.

In the same year Hugh Dalton – later to become a senior member of the Churchill and Attlee governments – issued his *With the British Guns in Italy*, in which the name Rinaldo Rinaldi appears. Hemingway may even have met the then Lieutenant Dalton, whose battery was positioned at a crossroads on the Altipiano of Asiago, which the American Red Cross ambulances passed every day as they picked up the wounded. Giovanni Cecchin has pointed out that another 1919 account of Caporetto, *La ritirata dal Friuli* by Ardengo Soffici, includes the story of a refugee who at a bridge on the Tagliamento was suspected of being a spy because of his foreign accent and dived into the river to escape arrest and execution.

The level of detail which Hemingway absorbed is extraordinary. Even in *Across the River and Into the Trees*, written over three decades later, his alter ego Richard Cantwell gives his driver Jackson an account of his youthful experiences on the frontline as they pass through San Dona, close to Fossalta, and reach a bridge over the Piave River: recalling the bloated bodies of dead soldiers floating in the water, and the difficulty of fighting in a flat landscape of ditches, hedgerows and canals, Cantwell recalls that the river had "very deep and tricky channels in the pebbles and shingles when it was shallow", adding, "There was a place called Grave di Papadopoli where it was plenty tricky".

Grave di Papadopoli may mean little or nothing to readers of Hemingway today – but it clearly meant a great deal to him, and indeed was a place all too familiar to those who lived through the Italian campaigns. An island in the Piave three miles long held by the Austrians as an advance post, it was overrun by the Italians (with British support) at the start of the final battle of Vittorio Veneto, marking the end of the war (and the collapse of the Austro-Hungarian Empire).

But then Hemingway's skill was to take the details of war and forge them into a gripping broader narrative. The story was so successful that it was filmed twice, in 1932 with Helen Hayes and Gary Cooper, and again in 1957 with Jennifer Jones and Rock Hudson. In *A Farewell to Arms* Frederic Henry says he is "always embarrassed by the words sacred, glorious and sacrifice". But at the time Hemingway felt buoyed up by his experiences, writing from his hospital bed after being wounded that he had looked death in the face and had witnessed "a great victory" on the Piave, which had shown the world what wonderful fighters the Italians were.

Although he and other Red Cross personnel were given nominal officer rank as lieutenants, Hemingway clearly felt discomfort at not having been an actual soldier involved in combat. This is clear from 'In Another Country', one of his stories about another Hemingway alter ego, Nick Adams, published in 1927 in the collection *Men Without Women*. Nick is not actually named in 'In Another Country', but it clearly belongs in the sequence and was included in the collection *The Nick Adams Stories* published by Charles Scribner's Sons in 1972 together with other war stories such as 'Night Before Landing', 'Now I Lay Me' and 'A Way You'll Never Be'.

In this story, narrated in the first person, Nick, like Hemingway himself, is a wartime ambulance driver being treated in hospital in Milan for leg injuries, with the army doctors proudly using up-to-date medical technology and experimental rehabilitation techniques. Nick suspects however that the photographs they are shown of recovered patients must have been manipulated since "I always understood we were the first to use the machines".

The hospital was "very old and very beautiful", Nick (or Hemingway) tells us, and when the street lights came on ("the dark came very early"), it was pleasant looking at the goods in shop windows and buying roasted chestnuts. But "it was a cold fall and the wind came down from the mountains". The officers moreover were disliked and resented in the "Communist quarter" of the city by townspeople who jostled them as they went by. Their refuge was (of course) the Cova, "next door to the Scala", where "the girls ... were very patriotic". "I found that the most patriotic people in Italy were the cafe girls", Nick says, adding "and I believe they are still patriotic".

Like Hemingway himself, Nick has been given medals, but feels that his fellow patients are worthier of recognition than he is: the citations, he feels, "really said, with the adjectives removed, that I had been given the medals because I was an American ... I had been wounded, it was true; but we all knew that being wounded, after all, was really an accident". For all his weaving of fact and fantasy, Hemingway is here being unduly harsh on himself (or at least on himself as Nick). As Fernanda Pivano, his Italian translator, once observed, "if there was one thing Hemingway did not lack it was courage". Courage, Hemingway famously remarked, amounted to "grace under pressure".

Even when Hemingway later settled at Key West in Florida – recommended to him by John Dos Passos – and in Cuba, the Italy of 1918 remained with him, and Nick Adams remained the persona through which he could deal with the traumas and neuroses which for all his bluster and bravado were the real legacy of his wartime experiences. In the case of the story 'Now I Lay Me', which like 'In Another Country' was published in 1927 as part of the *Men Without Women* collection, the legacy was insomnia.

The title derives from a familiar bedtime prayer for children first recorded in the eighteenth century:

Now I lay me down to sleep,
I pray the Lord my soul to keep,
His Love to guard me through the night,
And wake me in the morning's light.
Now I lay me down to sleep,
I pray the Lord my soul to keep,
If I should die before I wake,
I pray the Lord my soul to take.

Hemingway, however, was no doubt thinking of the First World War poster for US government bonds or 'Liberty Loans', which shows a little girl kneeling in prayer while her mother sits on the bed, above them a framed photograph of her older brother in uniform:

Now I lay me down to sleep,
I pray the Lord my soul to keep.
God bless my brother gone to war
Across the seas, in France, so far.
Oh, may his fight for Liberty
Save millions more than little me
From cruel fates or ruthless blast,
And bring him safely home at last.

On the surface 'Now I Lay Me' is a story about two army men, a lieutenant (addressed as 'Signor Tenente') and John, his Italian orderly from a Chicago family, sleeping – or rather, failing to sleep – in a tent, presumably a field hospital tent. Nick, or 'Signor Tenente', evidently with the child's verse in mind, is afraid to go to sleep while it is dark and so forces himself to stay awake: he is suffering from wounds and shell shock after a night bombing raid. The story is in effect a powerful interior monologue by Nick as he lies awake and runs memories through his brain, including the sound of silkworms – a reference to Villa Albrizzi, the silk warehouse at San Pietro Novello near Fossalta di Piave where Hemingway had spent nights at the front.

He tries to recall the names of birds, animals, food "and the names of all the streets I could remember in Chicago", but his mind strays to trout fishing, and then back to women: "Finally, though, I went back to trout fishing, because I found that I could remember all the streams and there was always something new about them, while the girls, after I had thought about them a few times, blurred and I could not call them into my mind and finally they all blurred and all became rather the same and I gave up thinking about them almost altogether."

Women nonetheless weigh heavily on Nick's consciousness, as indeed they did on Hemingway's. After the 'October offensive' – the Vittorio Veneto campaign – John visits the recovering Tenente at hospital in Milan "and was very disappointed that I had not yet married, and I know he would feel very badly if he knew that, so far, I have never married. He was going back to America and he was very certain about marriage and knew it would fix up everything."

'The Snows of Kilimanjaro' (1939) paints a memorable portrait of a writer recalling the Veneto battlefields of his youth such as the Pasubio mountains and the Asiago plateau as he lies dying in Africa. In Cuba in 1932, Hemingway wrote another of his 1918 Nick Adams stories, 'A Way You'll Never Be', the heat of Havana reminding him of "the way it was on the lower Piave in the summer of 1918". In this story Nick, distributing chocolates and cigarettes by bicycle like his creator, and wearing the same Spagnolini uniform, comes across the bodies of Austrians and Italians: "The hot weather had swollen them all alike regardless of nationality." They are surrounded by scattered belongings: helmets, gas masks, medical kits, photographs, letters. "There was always much paper about the dead and the debris of this attack was no exception."

At battalion headquarters Nick falls asleep and dreams of Fossalta di Piave: "Sometimes his girl was there and sometimes she was with someone else and he could not understand that, but those were the nights the river ran so much wider and stiller than it should and outside of Fossalta there was a low house painted yellow with willows all around it and a low stable and there was a canal..." For Hemingway it was a way of working through his war experiences, but also a way of reminding himself of the country he had left behind.

It is striking that several of the Nick Adams stories, written over a period of a decade or so, reflect not only Hemingway's time at the front as a teenager but also his doubts about marriage, which he evidently hoped would "fix up everything" but which repeatedly failed to do so. In 'In Another Country', a wounded Italian major whose hand has been reduced to a stump advises Nick never to get married, because it will only lead to him being hurt. "A man must not marry ... He should not place himself in a position to lose." Nick later learns from a doctor that the major's wife has died unexpectedly of pneumonia.

When November 1918 brought the end of the war at last, Hemingway wrote to his family: "Well it's all over! And I guess everybody is plenty joyous." The American hospitals in Italy were closing down, and it was time to "cross the ocean". His thoughts were turning to home. Despite the wounded major's words, Hemingway did now get married – although not to Agnes, nor to one of the Bellia girls he had met on the lake at Stresa, nor to the mysterious Maria from Turin. He met his wife in Chicago, and her name was Hadley.

9

Genoa Correspondent

"If you want to travel gaily, and I do, travel with good Italians"
Hemingway, *The Dangerous Summer*

H EMINGWAY RETURNED HOME in early January 1919, sailing
to New York from Genoa on the SS *Giuseppe Verdi*. He still
wore his splendid Spagnolini uniform and cape, and despite being
an aspiring author rather than an actual one – he was still not 20
years old – his impressive appearance made him a magnet for reporters who greeted Americans returning from the war. The *New York
Sun* interviewed Hemingway and printed a story about his frontline
wounds, saying he had "defied the shrapnel of the Central Powers".
He played on this image as a "war hero", even claiming that he had
been personally decorated by the King of Italy.

But the homecoming was also a time to catch his breath after
his Italian war experiences. He had survived not only operations on
his knees and legs but also the flu epidemic and bouts of jaundice,
tonsilitis and Vincent's angina, or "trench mouth". He was returning home to earn enough money to marry Agnes, who he habitually
referred to in letters as "my girl" and in a letter to his sister Marcelline in November 1918 simply called "the wife". And it was now that
he learned from Agnes that she was involved with someone else.

It remains unclear whether Agnes really ever thought of marrying him after the war: she referred to marriage several times in her letters, but later indicated she had only done so to stop Hemingway taking up Jim Gamble's offer, which would have made him a "kept man" travelling at someone else's expense. She was now at a hospital in Torre di Mosto, inland between Venice and the Adriatic coastal resort of Caorle, tending to wounded Italian soldiers.

"Dear Ernie, to me you are a wonderful boy", she wrote in January 1919. "I only fear all the Chicago femmes will be willing you away from your night nurse." But she was "not the perfect being you think I am", she wrote to Hemingway just two months later, in March 1919. Her feelings for him were more those of a mother than a sweetheart, and "I can't get away from the fact that you're just a boy – a kid". She was writing late at night after "a long think by myself", and "I am afraid it is going to hurt you".

Then came the revelation that she hoped to marry the aristocratic Italian officer Domenico Caracciolo, who she had nursed at Torre di Mosto. "I hope and pray that after you have thought things out, you'll be able to forgive me & start a wonderful career, & show what a man you really are. Ever admiringly and fondly, your friend, Aggie."

He took refuge in trying his hand at short stories, putting the finishing touches to 'The Mercenaries', in which he mocked the Italian daredevil pilot Fulco Ruffo di Calabria, possibly because it was the pilot's aunt, Rita Ruffo, a nursing colleague of Agnes', who had encouraged her to take up with Caracciolo. The year 1919 also saw 'The Passing of Pickles McCarty', at first called 'The Woppian Way' – Hemingway (in less generous moods) sometimes referred to Italy as 'Wopland', and the title is a play on the Appian Way.

"I hate jazzing all over Europe when there is so much of my own country I haven't seen", he wrote to a friend in Michigan in August 1920. "But the Wopland gets in the blood and kind of ruins you for anything else." The tale drew heavily on his time at Bassano del

Grappa and at the front with the Arditi. It tells the story of Nick Neroni, a boxer who changes his name to Pickles McCarty, volunteers to fight with the Arditi on the Italian front and then joins Gabriele D'Annunzio, the equally self-promoting Italian poet, flying ace and war hero, at Fiume.

Another tale told the story of the wartime misbehaviour of the fat, drunken and cowardly mayor of Roncade, which Hemingway described as a "hot white town" fifteen miles north of Venice, where "dusty trains of camions tore through the town bound for the front". 'How Death Sought Out the Town Major of Roncade' was only discovered in 2004 by the then mayor, Ivano Sartor, in the Hemingway archives at the Kennedy Library in Boston. It tells the story of a local man of noble origins named Vergara (we are not told his first name) who has pulled strings to get himself elected mayor (or 'major', after town officials were given military titles during the war).

Because the front is coming closer no one is left in Roncade except the mayor, the two young girls who run the trattoria and the whores at the Villa Rosa (brothel) who, however, are soon taken off to safety by a "smirking camion driver". Vergara, who had somehow imagined holding the top public office in the town would save him from the war, finds fear eating into his stomach "like a cancer" and takes refuge in cognac, sleeping it off in a room at the trattoria. When a Sardinian soldier arrives from the front and stops by for a drink, the cafe girls begin crying and tell him the mayor is a "lover of young girls".

The soldier finds the sleeping mayor, his "fat sensual lips" apart and his paunch moving "with every drunken breath", ties him to the bed and plants a hand grenade in the breast pocket of his pyjamas. When the mayor wakes up the soldier pulls the pin, telling the mayor it is time to face death "because of all the good men who have spilled out their guts along the Fossalta road while you have made love in Roncade". The story ends with the soldier confessing to his commanding officer that he "assisted" the mayor's death and asking to speak to a priest before returning to the frontline.

The magazines to which Hemingway sent his early stories replied with rejection slips, but he persisted, writing his first Nick Adams story, 'Big Two-Hearted River', a memorable account of his own trout fishing expeditions in Michigan, where Nick feels at home. Hemingway later commented that although the war is not mentioned in the story, it was about a young man recovering from wartime stress in the woods of his boyhood.

He also turned to poetry, in one poem taking a swipe at Gabriele D'Annunzio, even though he had at first admired D'Annunzio as a war hero and praised his novel *The Flame*. According to Giovanni Cecchin, the two men had even met, with documents found in the Hemingway papers at the Kennedy Library in Boston showing that in 1918 Hemingway and other Red Cross volunteers attended a religious ceremony for Italy's war dead at the Villa d'Orso (now the Hotel Selvatico) in Roncade at which D'Annunzio gave a patriotic address.

They may also have met at the officers mess at Ca' Morelli, a white-fronted eighteenth-century villa used during the war as a military hospital, and at the magnificent Castello di Roncade (or Villa Giustinian), which now offers fine wines, a luxury B&B and landscaped gardens decorated with sculptures, but which at the time was used as an Italian military command headquarters right on the frontline where D'Annunzio addressed the troops and their officers.

This, it seems, is the origin of a passage in Hemingway's much later Venice novel, *Across the River and Into the Trees*, in which Hemingway's alter ego, Colonel Cantwell, recalls seeing D'Annunzio giving troops a rousing speech at the Italian front in 1918 in pouring rain, one eye covered by a patch and his face "as white as the belly of a sole" and shouting *"morire non e basta"* ("to die is not enough" – though the Italian is not quite correct and D'Annunzio's slogan was actually slightly different, *morire non basta*). He also describes D'Annunzio as Jewish, which he was not.

On the Grand Canal in Venice Cantwell points out D'Annunzio's villa, saying "They loved him for his talent, and because he was bad, and he was brave ... He was a more miserable character than any that I know and as mean." In his contemptuous brief lampoon Hemingway now wrote: "Half a million dead wops/And he got a kick out of it/The son of a bitch." He again changed his mind a few years later however, writing in 1923 that D'Annunzio was an "old, bald-headed, perhaps a little insane but thoroughly sincere, divinely brave swashbuckler".

But in 1920 Hemingway was still a budding journalist, and his break came when in January he was invited to Toronto by Harriet Connable, a wealthy Michigan-born friend of his mother who had attended a talk which Hemingway gave to a ladies' charity in Petoskey about his wartime experiences. His job was to look after the Connables' invalid son Ralph Junior while Mrs Connable and her businessman husband Ralph (head of Woolworths in Canada) were on holiday in Florida. Mr Connable introduced Hemingway to editors at *The Toronto Star*, and he began writing features for their weekly magazine in 1920, the start of a relationship which would shortly lead to him becoming a *Toronto Star* foreign correspondent.

He was also a "free man" after Agnes' rejection, he told Jim Gamble, and therefore lucky – "tho of course I couldn't see it at the time". Back in Chicago he now met Elizabeth Hadley Richardson, a vivacious red-haired girl from St Louis, Missouri, who – like Agnes before her – was older than Hemingway, 29 to his 21. When they met through mutual friends at a party, Hemingway said, he knew at once that this was the girl he was destined to marry. She too was taken with this tall, handsome and well-built young man who had survived the war, "rocked on the balls of his feet", looked you straight in the eye while talking to you, and – like her – enjoyed a drink. They were married on 3 September 1921.

Hadley had income from a trust fund, which was useful since Hemingway was not at this stage making much money as a journalist. But he was writing and editing features for a monthly journal for Midwestern farmers called *The Co-operative Commonwealth*, and through this he met the well-known writer Sherwood Anderson, author of *Winesburg, Ohio*. Anderson suggested that the newlyweds should live not in America but in Europe, which was cheaper.

Hemingway was all for going back to Italy with his new bride – Naples, Capri and the Abruzzo were mentioned – but Anderson instead suggested Paris, recommending a left-bank hotel in Paris where he had himself lived for a time. He offered to give Hemingway introductions to Gertrude Stein, James Joyce, Ezra Pound and Sylvia Beach, literary patroness and owner of the celebrated book store Shakespeare and Company.

The newly married Hemingways sailed for Paris shortly before Christmas 1921 on the steamship *Leopoldina* and swiftly became part of the Parisian literary and artistic community. They met painters such as Joan Miro and Pablo Picasso, as well as writers such as Scott Fitzgerald and Gertrude Stein, who coined the phrase "the lost generation" for those who, like Hemingway, had spent their youthful years in the war. Stein became Hemingway's mentor (and later godmother to the Hemingways' son John Hadley Nicanor), although they eventually fell out. Ezra Pound Hemingway met in Sylvia Beach's bookshop, and Pound introduced him to James Joyce, with whom Hemingway enjoyed many an "alcoholic spree".

While in Paris Hemingway wrote features for the *Toronto Star*, and was not always complimentary about his fellow expats; an article on "American Bohemians in Paris" for example (25 March 1922) began "The scum of Greenwich Village, New York, has been skimmed off and deposited in large ladlesful on that section of Paris adjacent to the Cafe Rotonde", which was "the leading Latin Quarter show place for tourists in search of atmosphere".

But his career as a foreign correspondent really took off in April 1922, when the paper asked him to cover the post-war Genoa International Economic Conference of thirty-four nations, held in the great hall of the Palazzo San Giorgio. Its aim was to rebuild the global economy from the ruins of the First World War and negotiate both a return to the Gold Standard and some kind of economic understanding between the Western powers and the new Soviet government in Moscow.

He was back in Italy – indeed, in the very seaport from which he had sailed back to the US three years before. Genoa, once a city state rivalling Venice and known as "La Superba" because of its elegant sixteenth-century palazzos on the hill above the busy waterfront, would become something of a fixture later in his life as the port from which he regularly sailed to and from Havana. Hemingway is supposed to have described the monumental sculptures of Genoa's Staglieno cemetery above the city as "one of the wonders of the world", although no source has been found for this remark, and in *A Farewell to Arms* Genoa is described as "the place to see the bad marbles".

On his 1922 visit Hemingway for the first time encountered experienced old hands in the journalistic trade, including Max Eastman, Lincoln Steffens and Guy Hickok, with whom he would make a memorable tour of Italy five years later. He filed over fifteen reports from Genoa for the *Toronto Star*, describing for his readers a scene in the historic hall (site of the Banco San Giorgio, the oldest bank in the world) familiar to any journalist who has covered international gatherings. The delegates, he wrote, stood talking at the long table covered in white pads and inkwells because "they cannot find their place", while studying a quotation on the wall from Machiavelli, who had written "a book that could be used as a text book by all conferences".

There was also an enormous chandelier which blinded everyone in the press gallery, and marble effigies of the "swashbuckling pirates and traders that made Genoa a power in the old days when all the cities of Italy were at one another's throats". The official guests – white-moustachioed senators in top hats, women in Parisian hats and "wonderful, wealth-reeking fur coats" – sat behind in rows of camp chairs. "The fur coats are the most beautiful things in the hall."

Clearly more interested in people than economics, Hemingway spotted the Archbishop of Genoa in a red skull cap talking to an Italian general who looked like a "sunken-faced, kind-eyed Attila with his sweeps of moustaches". The press gallery filled up with correspondents (750 in a space reserved for 200): they were joined by the editor of the French Communist paper *L'Humanité*, who could afford to be a Communist because he had "a very rich wife".

The journalists identified the delegates for each other: the best-dressed were the British, headed by David Lloyd George, in his last months as prime minister. In the chair was the little-known Italian prime minister Luigi Facta – the last to hold that office before the March on Rome in October 1922 and the dictatorship of Benito Mussolini and the Fascists. Facta would try to stop Mussolini by declaring martial law, but King Victor Emmanuel III refused to sign the decree, appointing Mussolini prime minister when Facta resigned.

But that was still some six months away. At Genoa the main interest was in the four-man Soviet delegation, led by the "ham faced" Maxim Litvinov, Moscow's roving ambassador (and later foreign minister). Their chairs were at first empty: "the four emptiest looking chairs I have ever seen", Hemingway wrote.

They finally came in, followed by a mass of Russian secretaries, "far and away the best looking girls in the conference hall", and Signor Facta started the inevitable "dreary round of speeches". The Italian authorities meanwhile had mobilised 1500 military police to prevent violent clashes between Communists ("the Reds") and

Fascists ("a brood of dragon's teeth that were sown in 1920"): none of the police drafted in were from Genoa itself, "so they can shoot either side without fear or favour".

"I worked very hard at Genoa and wrote some very good stuff", Hemingway told his father, with some justification. Italy had claimed him again – and now that he was a married man he wanted to show Hadley *his* Italy, from Milan and the Dolomites to Rapallo. There was on the other hand the shadow of the "dragon's teeth", and in particular the rise of a fellow journalist, an Italian who, like Hemingway, had been wounded in the war but who – unlike Hemingway – had gone into politics: Benito Mussolini.

10

The Biggest Bluff in Europe

"Fascism is always made by disappointed people"
Hemingway to Bernard Berenson, March 1953

IN MAY 1922 Hemingway returned to Paris – but could not wait for Hadley to see Italy. The Hemingways headed first for the mountains of Switzerland, where they met up with his wartime friend Eric (Chink) Dorman-Smith, by now stationed in Germany, for some trout fishing.

They then – fuelled by brandy – planned to walk over the snow-covered St Bernard Pass into Italy. It was not perhaps the best way to introduce Hadley to *il bel paese*: they covered nearly sixty kilometres in two days, according to Hemingway, and by the time they reached Aosta his wife was hobbling badly, her feet covered in blisters because she was wearing fashionable Oxford shoes rather than boots. It was, according to Dorman-Smith, "something of a nightmare".

Hadley later blamed herself for "vanity and ignorance": the tan Oxfords, she said, were from Abercrombie and Fitch, and she had been showing off the shoes – and her legs – to Chink. Hemingway meanwhile had "bowel trouble" – a memory which stayed with him at least until 1954, when he wrote to Chink reminding him of their troubles crossing the St Bernard.

Hemingway was nonetheless undeterred. They took the train to Milan, and after Dorman-Smith had returned to Germany Hemingway proceeded to show Hadley the Milan he had got to know so well during his stay some four years earlier. "Wasn't it lovely coming down the Italian side and what fun we had in Aosta and then in Milano in the old Galleria", he wrote to Dorman-Smith. In his memoir *A Moveable Feast*, Hemingway recalls how Hadley later sought to put the painful memory of walking across the St Bernard in street shoes behind her ("My poor shoes"), preferring to remember Milan afterwards and "us having fruit cup at Biffi's in the Galleria with Capri and fresh peaches and wild strawberries in a tall glass pitcher with ice". The tour included not only Biffi's but also the other places he had shared so intimately with Agnes: the Duomo, the San Siro racetrack and the hospital where he had been operated on – though presumably he did not share with Hadley the memories of Agnes these conjured up.

He also wanted to show Hadley the spot where he had been wounded. They travelled first to Vicenza and Schio, up to Rovereto and Trento, then back down to Sirmione on Lake Garda, where they joined Ezra Pound and his wife Dorothy for some agreeable lakeside relaxation, including swimming and sunbathing. Only then did they take the train to Verona and change for Mestre, on the mainland opposite Venice, hiring a car and driver to take them from there to Fossalta di Piave.

Fossalta proved a great disappointment, at least for Hemingway: its "shattered, tragic dignity", he wrote, had been replaced by "a new, smug, hideous collection of plaster houses" in garish colours: the new "plaster church" was the worst. "A Veteran Visits The Old Front" was the headline on the piece he filed for the *Toronto Star*. "I had been in Fossalta perhaps fifty times and I would not have recognised it".

He found a rusting shell fragment on the grassy slope leading down to the Piave, but the shell scars on the trees had healed over. A village shattered by war, he said, always had a kind of dignity, "as though it had died for something" and as though better was to come. It was all part of a "great sacrifice". But now there was only the "new, ugly futility of it all". Everything was "just as it was – except a little worse", and a reconstructed town was much sadder than one that had been devastated.

It was altogether like going into an empty theatre after the audience and players had departed, with only the cleaners in the auditorium, Hemingway wrote. The trenches and shell holes had all been filled in, leaving the smooth green of the fields and "lonely, deadly dullness". Schio too had been a letdown: this "little town in the Trentino under the shoulder of the Alps" had once been "one of the finest places on earth", with "all the good cheer, amusement and relaxation a man could desire", to the point where he and his fellow Red Cross volunteers had thought it would be a wonderful place to live in after the war.

But it seemed to have mysteriously shrunk. The Albergo Due Spade (which Hemingway misspelt Spadi) was revealed to be no more than a rather shabby small inn, serving greasy food; the room where Hemingway and Hadley spent the night there had a squeaky bed which gave them a sleepless night (or so Hadley later complained). The wool factory and warehouse where Hemingway and his fellow volunteers had been billeted was back in action, creating "a flow of black muck polluting the stream where we used to swim".

The shop windows were full of fly-speckled pastries and cheap china dishes and postcards. Even the mountains appeared little more than mere hills compared to the great St Bernard Pass which he and Hadley had walked over the week before. When he told the girl serving at the local bar that he had been in Schio during the war, she replied with indifference: "So were many others".

He remembered with nostalgia the garden in which he and his

fellow American volunteers had drunk beer on hot nights, with a plane tree overhead and wisteria on the walls, but after his afternoon walk decided not to try and find it after all. "Maybe there never was a garden. Perhaps there never was any war around Schio at all". He would "give a lot not to have gone". The train back to Venice, which he and Hadley could see "way off across the swamp" like "a fairy city", was equally disillusioning, the carriage full of "evil-smelling Italian profiteers going to Venice for vacations".

The drive from Mestre, where they hired a car and driver, was another letdown, the route taking them past the "poisonous green Adriatic marshes", where the car at one point broke down. "I had tried to recreate something for my wife and had failed utterly", Hemingway wrote. The moral was: "don't go back". "For Christ's sake don't ever go back Horney", he wrote later to his friend Bill Horne, who was also from Chicago and had shared his frontline experiences, including the nights at the silkworm warehouse at Monastier.

Hemingway recalled the days of lost innocence when they had first arrived at Schio on a hot day in June "and we didn't know what it would be like except that they had a place to swim and all drove Fiats". Now it was "all gone and Italy is all gone ... We can't ever go back to old things or try and get the old kick out of something or find things the way we remembered them. We have them as we remember them and they are very fine and wonderful and we have to go on and have other things because the old things are nowhere except in our minds now."

Back in Paris there were other tensions. When Hemingway was assigned by his paper to cover the Lausanne peace conference called in November 1922 to revise the harsh terms imposed on Turkey after the First World War and the collapse of the Ottoman Empire, Hadley travelled by train to join him – and at the Gare de Lyon lost a suitcase containing nearly all the manuscripts of the short stories he had begun to write.

Hemingway and his wife also fell out when the *Toronto Star* asked him to cover the Greco-Turkish war: she begged him not to go, but he went anyway. The plight of Greek refugees he witnessed in Thrace haunted him for years afterward. The war had begun with the collapse of the Ottoman Empire in 1918, when Lloyd George and the Allies promised Greece territorial gains at Turkey's expense.

Greek forces occupied Smyrna (now Izmir) in 1919 and then much of Anatolia, which had a sizeable Greek Orthodox population. Greece was not making war on Islam, the Greek prime minister Eliftherios Venizelos insisted, only on the anachronistic Ottoman system. The Turks however – led by the charismatic Mustafa Kemal (Atatürk) – counter-attacked, and by 1922 had re-taken the territory, including Constantinople as well as Smyrna, where the Great Fire of September 1922 destroyed much of the historic port.

It was a bitter struggle in which both sides committed atrocities. Hemingway was particularly moved by the plight of Greek Christian refugees in Eastern Thrace as they moved slowly across the Maritza River at Adrianople (now Edirne) near the Bulgarian border in pouring rain, a twenty-mile column of "exhausted, staggering men, women and children, blankets over their heads" accompanied by bullocks, muddy-flanked water buffalo, chickens and all "their worldly goods". It was a "ghastly, shambling procession of people being driven from their homes", he reported for the *Star* in November 1922.

Sleeping on cold floors and bitten by mosquitoes in the "black, slippery, smelly offal-strewn streets of Constantinople" (the "magic of the East" described by Pierre Loti, he wrote, had to be balanced by the reality of poverty and mud), Hemingway contracted malaria, dosing himself with aspirin and quinine washed down with "sickly sweet Thracian wine". Still feverish, he trudged along with the refugees, "dodging camels that swayed and grunted along, past flat-wheeled ox carts piled high with bedding, mirrors, furniture, pigs tied flat, mothers huddled under blankets with their babies, old men and women leaning on the back of the buffalo carts and just keeping their feet moving, their eyes on the road and their heads sunken".

His mood of disillusionment was reinforced by the rise of Mussolini and Fascism in Italy. While showing Hadley round Milan he had requested an interview with Mussolini and been granted access to the Fascist leader at the offices of the newspaper Mussolini founded and edited, *Il Popolo d'Italia*. He was charmed, as many foreign correspondents were, by the future dictator. Possibly Hemingway was influenced by the fact that Mussolini, like himself, had been wounded at the front during the recent war, in his case on the Slovenian border not far from Gorizia. At 39, however, Mussolini was considerably older than Hemingway, who was still only 23 and perhaps over-impressed.

Mussolini, who fondled the ears of an enormous pet wolfhound during the interview, was a big man with a high forehead, a slow-smiling mouth and "expressive hands". He was not the monster he had pictured but a patriot, Hemingway thought – though questions had been raised about how he would use his growing power as his Fascist party became a "military force" half a million strong. "We have force enough to destroy any government that might try to oppose or destroy us", Mussolini declared to Hemingway.

If Hemingway had any illusions about Mussolini, however, he had lost them by the time he came to cover the Lausanne conference, held at the neo-Gothic Chateau de Ouchy (now a hotel), a venue "so ugly that it makes the Odd Fellows Hall of Petoskey, Michigan, look like the Parthenon". Ouchy (pronounced Ooshy, Hemingway helpfully informed his readers) was no longer the lakeside fishing village it had been when Byron visited it but full of "enormous, empty hotels" with "lines of limousines" for the delegates.

Mustafa Kemal was impressive, with "a face that no one can forget", although Ismet Pasha, head of the Turkish delegation, was

"absolutely without magnetism", with "a face no one can remember".
He interviewed Ismet – "we got along very well, as we both spoke
such bad French" – and also observed him at a jazz club smiling
delightedly at the dancers and eating "quantities of cakes" and telling
the waitress "countless jokes in bad French".

But at least Ismet was "genuine" whereas Mussolini, by now in
power in Rome, was "the biggest bluff in Europe. If Mussolini would
have me taken out and shot tomorrow morning I would still regard
him as a bluff. The shooting would be a bluff." Mussolini had a weakness of the mouth which gave him the famous scowl imitated by
every 19-year-old Fascist in Italy; his propensity for duels was also a
sign of weakness and cowardice, since "really brave men do not have
to fight duels, and many cowards duel constantly to make themselves believe they are brave".

There was also "something wrong, even histrionically, with a man
who wears white spats with a black shirt". The Fascist leader might,
Hemingway conceded, become "a great and lasting force", but it was
"a very dangerous thing to organise the patriotism of a nation if you
are not sincere", especially if you ask people to donate money to the
cause, as Mussolini had, because "once the Latin has sunk his money
in a business he wants results".

Ultimately, Hemingway believed, Mussolini was a fraud – and
he had the proof. "The Fascist dictator had announced he would
receive the press. Everybody came. We all crowded into the room."
Mussolini was sitting at his desk reading a book, his face contorted in
his famous frown: "he was registering Dictator". As an ex-newspaper
man, Hemingway suggested, Mussolini was aware how many readers
would be reached by the accounts of the 200 or so correspondents
in the room and was imagining their opening lines – something like
"As we entered the room the Black Shirt Dictator did not look up
from the book he was reading, so intense was his concentration".
Hemingway then tiptoed over behind the Duce (or so he claimed)

"to see what the book was he was reading with such avid interest. It was a French-English dictionary – held upside down".

Hemingway's view of Mussolini darkened further in later years. He was appalled by the assassination in 1924 of the Socialist opposition deputy Giacomo Matteoti, "one of the most horrible crimes ever committed by any government", as he wrote to Ernest Walsh, and by the dropping the following year of all charges against Matteoti's Fascist killers. The Italians were "worse crooks than the French" and he could not go back to live in Italy "because the political situation makes me so furious". It was "awfully discouraging to think that the country that produced Garibaldi should be ruled by that horrible gang".

By the time he came to write his introduction to the anthology *Men At War* during the Second World War, he no longer believed the legend of Mussolini's bravery when wounded on the Carso during the First World War. Instead (unlike, by implication, his own behaviour) Mussolini had used "martial bombast and desire for military glory" to cover up the fact that he had been frightened by the fighting and had made an "ignominious exit" from it "at the first opportunity".

"Mussolini I knew fairly well", he wrote to the art critic Bernard Berenson in 1953. "When you had known a wicked old man like Clemenceau, Mussolini was not very interesting", he added dismissively. It was impossible not to remember the Duce "as a coward in the war and as a crooked journalist".

11

Rapallo and Cortina

"After renouncing Italy and all its works I've gotten all nostalgique about it. I bet it's swell now"

Hemingway to Ezra Pound, 17 March 1924

RAPALLO TODAY STILL conjures up a vision of seaside charm. It boasts a sixteenth-century sea fortress, the Castello sul Mare, built to defend the town against Turks and pirates when it was still part of the Republic of Genoa, and elegant villas set in the hillside above the promenade. Rapallo has inspired writers, thinkers and artists including Friedrich Nietzsche, Ezra Pound and Max Beerbohm, the caricaturist, who lived there from 1910 onwards (and died in Rapallo in 1956), with the celebrated stage designer Gordon Craig in the villa next door from 1917 to 1928. After the war it was the scene of an international conference which drew up the 1920 Treaty of Rapallo, resolving frontier issues between Serbia, Croatia and Slovenia.

Henry Villard, who had met Hemingway when they were both at the American Red Cross hospital in wartime Milan, later recalled having suggested Rapallo to him as a place to relax or convalesce. Its attractions, Villard said, included swimming off the rocks, an English-speaking contessa to dance with against "an unreal background of music, moonlight and roses", and cherry brandy and crème de menthe after dinner "to complement the miniature port and starboard lights of the vessels manoeuvring offshore".

Hemingway had made his first visit to Rapallo during the 1922 Genoa conference, with other reporters, to interview the Russian delegates who were staying there. But he also went there as a welcome break from covering the talks to meet Max Beerbohm, driving past hillsides of vines and olive groves together with two other journalists, Max Eastman, the left-wing (at the time) editor of the socialist magazine *The Masses*, and George Slocombe of the London *Daily Herald*.

Beerbohm had left the bustle of literary and political London for Liguria, preferring the peace and quiet of the orange and lemon trees in his garden and the Mediterranean views he could see from the cane chair on his terrace at the Villino Chiaro. He received few guests, but agreed to meet the Genoa journalists, offering them Marsala and discussing the need for creative artists to "revolt against the evils of commercial journalism".

The following year Hemingway had an even more pressing reason to go to Rapallo: Ezra and Dorothy Pound had moved there after Hemingway had sung its praises to them. Ernest and Hadley – who was by now pregnant – stayed at the Hotel Splendide in February and March 1923. The Hemingways had got to know Ezra and Dorothy Pound well in Paris, and had enjoyed a brief holiday with them on Lake Garda.

Pound – who was 14 years older than Hemingway – had encouraged the younger man's attempts to write fiction, while Hemingway greatly admired the American poet's work. He also tried to teach Pound how to box, but found – as he told Sherwood Anderson – that the poet "led with his chin" and had "the grace of a crayfish". "I was never able to teach him to throw a left hook", he recalled later in his memoir *A Moveable Feast*.

At one stage Pound annoyed Hemingway by disappearing to Rome during the Hemingways' visit. There were complications in Pound's private life: he had just met the American violinist Olga Rudge, who would be his mistress for half a century. Olga followed him to Rapallo, and in 1925 had his daughter Mary (now Mary de Rachewitz, for many years curator of the Ezra Pound Archives at Yale University). Dorothy at this stage was trying to turn a blind eye to Ezra's affair.

Perhaps because of Pound's erratic behaviour, Hemingway was in a jaundiced mood, and – even though he had himself recommended it to Ezra and Dorothy – refused to be impressed by Rapallo. "The place ain't much", he wrote to Gertrude Stein in Paris on 23 February 1923. The weather was muggy and humid, and the Mediterranean "weak and dull". It was a quiet place, according to WB Yeats, another writer who sought the sun there, with no great casino or ballroom and no great harbour full of yachts.

Hemingway wrote a sketch called 'Rapallo' in which he said he and his wife were happy "sometimes", and were "happiest in bed". He also wrote 'Cat in the Rain', a sketch about an American couple in a room on the second floor of a hotel facing the sea, the public garden and the war memorial, where they "did not know any of the people they passed on the stairs on their way to and from their room ... In the good weather there was always an artist with his easel. Artists liked the way the palms grew and the bright colors of the hotels facing the gardens and the sea."

The wife – who is not named, but is presumably based on Hadley – wants a stable rather than transient life: she yearns for "a kitty to sit on my lap and purr when I stroke her", a sign perhaps of her longing for a baby. She wants "to eat at a table with my own silver and I want candles. And I want it to be spring and I want to brush my hair out in front of a mirror and I want a kitty and I want some new clothes." The wife sees a cat sheltering from the rain under a green table in the garden, and goes downstairs to rescue it, but it has disappeared. The husband, George, is indifferent, telling her at one point to "shut up and get something to read".

This is a fairly bleak portrait of a marriage, and while it need not be read as a literal account of Hemingway's relationship with Hadley, it almost certainly reflects tensions below the surface – an early example of Hemingway's "iceberg" theory of fiction, in which more is going on than the spare details at first seem to indicate. He used the same technique in his 1927 story 'Hills Like White Elephants', in which an American and his girlfriend waiting at a Spanish railway station discuss whether or not she should have an "operation" – without mentioning the word abortion.

No doubt Hemingway was still smarting from the loss of his suitcase of stories. But he was determined to start making a living from fiction rather than journalism, and was cheered up when Pound introduced him to Edward O'Brien, the Boston-based anthologist and compiler of short stories, who at the time was staying – as Hemingway recalls in *A Moveable Feast* – "as a boarder in a monastery up above Rapallo".

O'Brien was actually staying at a hostel next door to the Sanctuary of Our Lady of Montallegro, where the Virgin Mary had appeared to a local peasant in the sixteenth century. Two kilometres north of Rapallo and 600 metres above sea level, and nowadays reached by a cable car (*funivia*), the sanctuary offers spectacular views of the Gulf of Tigullio on the Mediterranean below. Here Hemingway showed O'Brien his story 'My Old Man', which had escaped Hadley's disaster at the Gare de Lyon. O'Brien, who normally only accepted already published stories for his anthologies, made an exception and included it in *Best American Short Stories of 1923*.

To cheer him further Pound, who was composing his cantos on Sigismondo Malatesta, the fifteenth-century nobleman and *condottiere* known as 'the Wolf of Rimini', suggested a walking tour of places linked to Malatesta's turbulent life as a warlord and military commander. Hemingway hesitated, saying he had little idea who Malatesta was and "no wish to eat bad food and sleep in poor inns in Italy in February".

But they set off anyway, and Hemingway duly enjoyed hiking with a rucksack through vineyards and olive groves toward Pisa and Siena, discussing Malatesta's campaigns at Piombino and Orbetello with Pound during picnics of cheese, figs and wine. "Ezra's knowledge of Italian and Italian people and Italian history shone brilliantly amongst those gorgeous old ruins", Hadley remarked – though she was irritated that Pound seemed interested only in Hemingway and paid no attention to her.

The trip remained in Hemingway's memory over twenty years later, when his fourth wife Mary was considering a visit to Orbetello, though in his mind it was by now he and not Pound who had displayed knowledge of Italian history: "I walked all over that country with Ezra explaining him how and why Sigismundo Malatesta would have fought where and for what reasons and how would have worked", he wrote to her in November 1948 from the Locanda Cipriani on Torcello in the Venetian lagoon, somewhat ungrammatically (due no doubt to having lunched "outdoors in the sun".) He added: "Probably mis-led him badly. Would like to do it better now."

After the Orbetello trip the Pounds returned to Rapallo while the Hemingways travelled by train to Milan and then up to the mountain resort of Cortina d'Ampezzo in Hemingway's beloved Veneto, staying for nearly three weeks, from 10 to 30 March 1923. Cortina d'Ampezzo, nowadays known simply as Cortina, was at that time – and still is – a fashionable and chic ski resort favoured by the rich and aristocratic, set 4000 feet above sea level in an Alpine valley of the Dolomites.

It had been Austrian until the First World War, when it passed to Italy. "Cortina d'Ampezzo is the swellest country on earth",

Hemingway wrote to Ernest Walsh in 1925. "It is the loveliest country I've ever known." The Hemingways stayed in the elegant Hotel Bellevue, and frequented the bar at the Hotel Posta (now the Hotel de la Poste). Hemingway began to get to know local society – including Dora Ivancich, the future mother of Adriana, the teenage girl he would fall in love with over twenty years later and the inspiration for *Across the River and Into the Trees*, and Dora's sister-in-law Emma.

The holiday was once again interrupted by journalism however, this time an urgent request from the *Toronto Star* to cover Franco-German tensions in the Ruhr valley, centre of the German coal and steel industries, which French and Belgian troops had occupied as retaliation for the failure of the Weimar Republic to honour reparations agreed after the First World War. It was not an easy assignment: as he reported to readers, he first had to obtain a visa to enter Germany, which was reluctantly granted by the German consul in Paris after Hemingway had provided a letter from the US Embassy "printed on stiff crackling paper and bearing an enormous red seal".

Hadley (who by now had proper mountain boots) stayed on at Cortina with her new friend Renata Borgatti, the pianist and Lesbian lover of Faith Mackenzie, the bisexual wife of the novelist Compton Mackenzie. She was amusing company, and at concerts often accompanied Olga Rudge, Pound's mistress. Hadley and Renata became close friends, though not anything more intimate: when Hadley suggested to Renata that she should try men rather than women as lovers, remarking "You don't know what you're missing", Renata replied, "But Hadley, you don't know what *you're* missing".

Hemingway returned from the Ruhr in April, telling his father in a letter that he was getting tired of so much travelling. He was also getting tired of Italy: it was now that he warned Bill Horne, the Chicago friend who had served with him in the American Red

Cross at Schio, not to go back, saying Italy was "all gone". His mood was probably darkened by an unpleasant episode in Cortina: since the snow was melting Hemingway hired a guide to go fishing, but the guide – who was drunk – failed to inform him that fishing was illegal. Hemingway transformed this experience into the story 'Out Of Season', later published in the collection *In Our Time*, in which a husband and wife fall out over a disastrous fishing expedition.

After Cortina, Hemingway and Hadley went first to Spain to witness the running of the bulls at Pamplona, and then in August they sailed to Quebec from Cherbourg on the Cunard line *Andania*. From Quebec they headed for Toronto, where Hemingway resumed his career as a reporter for the *Star* and where in October 1923 their son John Hadley Nicanor was born, named after his mother and a Spanish bullfighter Hemingway had admired.

Spain was to be one of the great loves of his life, and would produce *The Sun Also Rises*, *Death in the Afternoon* and *For Whom the Bell Tolls*. He was increasingly disillusioned with the Italy of Mussolini and his "government by lead pipe and castor oil", a reference to the brutal methods used by Mussolini's Blackshirts to intimidate opponents such as beating them and forcing several pints of castor oil down their throats to cause dehydration and severe diarrhoea. "I've buried Italy, and why dig it up when there's a chance it still stinks?" he said at one point.

But several of the stories he was writing, such as 'A Way You'll Never Be' and 'In Another Country' were set in the Italy of 1918, and he was beginning to draft ideas for what would become *A Farewell to Arms*. In March 1924 he admitted to Pound that even though he had "renounced Italy and all its works", he remained nostalgic for it (he even wrote "homesick", but crossed it out). And in 1927 he returned with his friend and fellow journalist Guy Hickok for one more "bachelor trip" as he divorced the long-suffering Hadley and prepared to marry his second wife, Pauline Pfeiffer.

12

Che Ti Dice La Patria?

"Mussolini told me at Lausanne, you know, that I couldn't ever live in Italy again"

Hemingway to Ezra Pound, 23 January 1923

THE TORONTO INTERLUDE did not last long: Hemingway found that the life of a journalist in Canada was not only boring but involved excessively long hours, and he resigned from the *Star*. He, Hadley and baby John (known as Jack, or 'Bumby') returned to Paris at the start of 1924, with Hemingway writing for *The Transatlantic Review*, a short-lived magazine backed by Ezra Pound and edited by Ford Madox Ford. The Hemingways made several more trips to Pamplona, resulting in *The Sun Also Rises* (published in London under the title *Fiesta*), which Hemingway dedicated to Hadley and their son.

The fact was however that they were drifting apart, and Hemingway had started an affair with the wealthy Pauline Pfeiffer, known as Fife, a journalist for *Vogue* magazine in Paris who had got to know them both in Paris and Antibes, accompanied them to Pamplona and Austria, and set out to befriend Hadley – all while seducing Ernest. She invited them to expensive restaurants, knowing Hadley could not leave Bumby behind, and took Hemingway back to her apartment, with inevitable results.

Hemingway was not immediately attracted to Pauline: looking back on the affair much later, he told AE Hotchner that after first meeting Pauline over dinner at the Fitzgeralds' flat in Paris he had not given her another thought. Hadley was "the only woman who mattered in my life", with her "full body and full breasts", wearing little or no jewellery or make up. Pauline by contrast was "small and flat-chested" with close cropped hair "like a boy's", bright red rouged lips and loops of pearls and costume jewellery. Where Hadley was straightforward, Pauline was a "schemer".

She had, Hemingway told Hotchner, "the 'I get what I want' hubris of a very rich girl who won't be denied". "You're being set up by a femme fatale", Scott Fitzgerald warned Hemingway: Pauline was "shopping for a husband" and would "do anything" to get him. When Hemingway replied that he was in love with two women at the same time Fitzgerald replied that "a man torn between two women will eventually lose them both". "She's going to bust up your marriage if you don't get rid of her", he told Hemingway bluntly.

Hadley suspected what was going on. When she asked Pauline's equally glamorous sister Virginia (known as Ginny, or Jinny) whether Hemingway and Pauline were in love, Ginny replied cautiously "I think they are very fond of each other", which only confirmed Hadley's fears. She came to regret that she had not told Pauline bluntly to "leave my husband alone" instead of tolerating what amounted to a *menage a trois*. "I should have said to her 'No, you can't have my husband'", Hadley told her friend and first biographer Alice Sokoloff many years later. "But I didn't."

Hemingway also knew what was going on, and came to regret leaving "lovely Hadley" (who swiftly re-married) for Pauline. Looking back years later in his memoir *A Moveable Feast* he described Pauline's behaviour as "the oldest trick there is. It is that an unmarried young woman becomes the temporary best friend of another young woman who is married, goes to live with the husband and wife and then unknowingly, innocently and unrelentingly sets out to marry the husband." It was a "trick" which Martha Gellhorn, Hemingway's third wife, would use later on when she in turn replaced Pauline – in both cases the words "unknowingly" and "innocently" are perhaps misplaced.

In the 1920s Hemingway, as Naomi Wood puts it in *Mrs Hemingway*, her recent fictionalised account of the affair, was fit, bronzed and handsome – so much so that even his male friends were "bowled over by his looks". He was changeable in mood, meek at one time and bullish, even violent at another. But it was "shocking what he can get away with": women "snap their heads to watch him go and they don't stop looking until he's gone". He nonetheless came to regret losing Hadley: he genuinely loved Pauline, he told his father in 1927, but if Hadley had said she wanted him back after their divorce, "I would have gone back to her".

Hemingway and Hadley separated in the summer of 1926. Hadley told Hemingway she would agree to a divorce if he and Pauline kept apart for a hundred days and still felt the same way about each other, but in the end she gave in before the period was up. She and Hemingway were divorced in January 1927, with Hemingway offering Hadley the royalties from *The Sun Also Rises* as part of the divorce agreement. He then married Pauline in May.

But before doing so he set off with Guy Hickok, who was Paris bureau chief for the *Brooklyn Daily Eagle*, in Hickok's battered old Ford coupe – known as Henry – with a cracked windscreen on a ten-day tour of Italy. On the surface it was a pre-wedding bachelor trip, or what Pauline called "an Italian tour for the promotion of masculine society". But Hickok had told Hemingway in January that he wanted to go to Italy to "write some silly stuff about Fascism".

A week later he urged Hemingway to pack a bag "and take the other seat in my Henry – assuming he hasn't fallen apart by then". He wanted to "splutter down to Rimini" and "sizzle", and then "spit up to San Remo" on the way back. Hemingway replied that he thought he could remember enough Italian to get them petrol and oil, and beds at hotels along the way, and that Ezra Pound had written to say he was looking forward to seeing them both in Rapallo.

Hickok was mainly interested in San Marino – "We could do anything you please as long as San Marino was on the way" – and suggested they could also revisit the sites in the Veneto where Hemingway had been on the frontline. "I know how all the soldier boys love their old fronts." But Hemingway had already made that pilgrimage with Hadley, and had other stops in mind during the trip, during which Hickok drove 3000 kilometres at 15–20 miles an hour in the old Ford while Hemingway navigated. He also interpreted for Hickok, who had good French (he had set up the *Brooklyn Daily Eagle* bureau in Paris in 1918) but no Italian.

They drove from Paris down the Rhone Valley to the French-Italian border on the Riviera, Hemingway related in 'Italy 1927', his account of the trip for *The New Republic*. From Ventimiglia they motored on 18 March to Rapallo, La Spezia, Pisa and Florence, and then across the Romagna to San Marino and Rimini, where Hemingway picked up letters from Pauline at the once luxurious Grand Hotel Aquila D'Oro (now municipal offices, with only the splendid facade remaining). Hemingway and Hickok then drove up the Adriatic coast to Forli and back in a loop through Imola, Bologna, Parma and Piacenza to Genoa and Ventimiglia.

The trip enabled Hemingway to take up the invitation to call once again on Ezra and Dorothy Pound at Rapallo: he and Hickok (whose name Hemingway consistently misspells as 'Hickock') were heading for Rimini and San Marino in March, he wrote to Pound in February 1927, and hoped to meet up either on the way there or on the way back. In fact they had dinner with the Pounds on the outward journey, on Friday 18 March, their first day in Italy, and no doubt discussed Pound's new magazine *Exile* – both Hemingway and Hickok were among the contributors that year to the first edition, issued that very month. Hickok, who was 11 years older than the 27-year-old Hemingway and something of a mentor to the younger journalist, wrote a waspish portrait of Pound in the sketches of their trip he published the following month in *The Brooklyn Eagle*, mocking Pound's patronage of "unknown writers" in his "queer little short-lived magazines" with "circulations numbering only a few hundreds".

Pound, Hickok said, had a reputation as an eccentric because of his reddish beard and his velvet coats, although Pound claimed they had been given to him by "would-be Bohemian Americans who hadn't the courage to wear them after they had bought them for their own use". Pound had published his Malatesta cantos in expensive editions, writing them in a mixture of Italian, Latin and modern slang, and had staged concerts in Paris by "grand opera singers" of "forgotten songs of the medieval troubadours".

Part of the "Pound enigma", Hickok suggested, was that all this cost him money. He often turned out to be right on the other hand, and "a surprising number of persons whose things appeared in his little magazines and booklets when they were totally unknown have since gained international recognition" – writers such as DH Lawrence, James Joyce, TS Eliot and a certain Ernest Hemingway. Besides, Pound had a "regular bathtub", which was apparently not easy to find in Italy, a "very charming wife" in Dorothy, and he had paid for dinner, which Hickok concluded ironically meant that "we decided the stop might be called a pilgrimage. Had he not done so we would have merely said that we stumbled on him there while passing through on more important business."

In his own account of the trip, published in May, a month after Hickok's pieces appeared, Hemingway did not mention the visit to Pound in Rapallo, focusing instead on life under Fascism. There had been – he wrote rather defensively – no opportunity "in such a short trip" to "see how things were with the country or the people". He did however offer a reportage which amounted to the same thing – although his vignettes did not perhaps give the negative impression of Fascism he was trying to convey.

En route to the port of La Spezia on a Sunday they came to Carrodano, a village of white-painted houses surrounded by vines where the men were playing bowls in their Sunday best. In the main piazza they were approached by a young man carrying a suitcase who "came up to the car and asked us to take him in to Spezia". When Hemingway pointed out there were only two seats in the car, and both were occupied, the man explained that he was a Fascist and was used to travelling in discomfort. Without being asked he climbed onto the running board, "holding on inside, his right arm through the open window". The air was frosty but "the young man projected from the side of the car like the figurehead of a ship. He had turned his coat collar up and pulled his hat down and his nose looked cold in the wind."

As the car was descending toward La Spezia the young Fascist asked to be set down, explaining that if he went with them into the town they might get into trouble for carrying passengers. He offered to pay them for the lift, but when told it was free said "thanks" and "looked after us suspiciously as Guy started the car. I waved my hand at him. He was too dignified to reply. We went on into Spezia. 'That's a young man that will go a long way in Italy,' I said to Guy. 'Well,' said Guy, 'he went twenty kilometres with us.'"

The sketch does not quite come off however, since the Fascist appears in quite a good light. Hemingway notes that "thanks" was inadequate, since in Italy "thank you very much" or "thanks a thousand times" (*grazie mille*) is normal for even the smallest favour. On the other hand the young man must have seemed to some readers at least to be polite (he offered to pay), hardy (standing on the running board) and even considerate (not wanting them to be caught carrying a passenger). The same could be said of his second vignette, 'A Meal in Spezia', revealing that because Mussolini had closed down Italian brothels, prostitutes were doubling as waitresses and entertaining clients in the back rooms of restaurants instead.

Among the "high and yellow" houses of La Spezia, their walls stencilled with "eye-bugging portraits of Mussolini", they found a modest restaurant near the harbour with a sailor and a smartly dressed young man in a blue suit sitting at tables and three girls and an old woman at another table. One of the girls, Hemingway tells us, took their order (spaghetti and red wine), putting her arm round Hickok's neck, while another stood in the doorway, the light making clear that "she was wearing nothing under her house dress".

The waitress who had taken their order "put her hands on her breasts and smiled" and asked Hickok if he liked her. The girl had taken them for Germans, and Hemingway played along, saying they were from Potsdam. He mocks the girl's nose and general appearance – "she smiled better on one side than the other" – and after she has offered herself to an embarrassed Hickok ("Tell him he is mine ... Tell him he is a beautiful boy") the two men leave, telling the disappointed girls that they have to get to Pisa and Florence. They pay the bill and leave a tip, but the general impression (presumably not intended by Hemingway) is that it is he who behaves badly, not the girls. They wave when the car starts, but the girl in the doorway – not surprisingly – does not wave back.

A restaurant also features in 'After the Rain', the third sketch of 'Italy 1927', when Hemingway and Hickok reach the suburbs of Genoa in pouring rain, with the trucks splashing "liquid mud" onto pedestrians on the pavements. "On our left was the Mediterranean. There was a big sea running and waves broke and the wind blew the spray against the car."

They stop for lunch at Sestri – *pasta asciutta* (pasta with a meat and basil sauce, the meal Frederic Henry is eating at the battlefront with cheese and wine when he is wounded in *A Farewell to Arms*) – followed by steak and fried potatoes, but "there was no heat in the restaurant and we kept our hats and coats on." The pasta was good, we are told, but "the wine tasted of alum, and we poured water in it".

After the meal Hickok is taken to a nearby house to use the toilet, there being none in the restaurant, but "the people in the house were suspicious and the waiter had remained with Guy to see nothing was stolen". Back on the road Hemingway remarks that the poet Shelley was drowned "somewhere along here", only to be reminded by Hickok that Shelley drowned further down the coast at Viareggio. In the final incident of the narrative, they pass "a Fascist riding a bicycle, a heavy revolver in a holster on his back" who joins them as they wait at a railway level crossing and offers to clean their dirty licence plate for them.

Hemingway points out that he had cleaned the plate himself back at Sestri, and insists it is readable. "It's only dirty from the state of the roads", he tells the Fascist. "You don't like Italian roads?" "They are dirty." "Fifty lire." He spat in the road. "Your car is dirty and you are dirty, too." "Good. And give me a receipt with your name."

The Fascist – presumably a policeman – fines them fifty lire for having a dirty licence plate, at first handing them a receipt for only twenty-five lire, which Hemingway spots. The policeman "smiled a beautiful Italian smile and wrote something on the receipt stub, holding it so I could not see. "Go on", he said, "before your number gets dirty again".

In his own sketches of the trip Hickok reports another row with a Fascist official, this time a militiaman who fined them for failing to stop at a railway crossing and nearly colliding with a train. Hickok was baffled by the variety of police, militia and army uniforms, but Hemingway, who had "fought the war in some of them", put him straight. In fact Hemingway, Hickok adds – perhaps slightly irritated by his companion's know-it-all manner – "used to know

Mussolini" and had predicted the Duce's March on Rome a year and half before it happened, "but then nobody believed him".

In contrast to Mussolini's Italy, France, after they had crossed back over the border and reached Menton, seemed "very cheerful and clean and sane and lovely", Hemingway wrote. The Ford eventually broke down, as Hickok had predicted, but by then they were near Dijon, and Hemingway could take the train back to Paris. When his account of the Italian tour was later included in his collection *Men Without Women*, he re-titled it 'Che Ti Dice La Patria?', a patriotic slogan of D'Annunzio's – best translated in this context perhaps as 'What Does Your Country Mean To You?', though Hemingway himself suggested 'What Do You Hear From Home?' or 'What Doth the Fatherland Say To Thee?' in a letter to his editor, Maxwell Perkins. The phrase was used in leaflets dropped to Italian troops by air, together with the answer "*Tiene Duro*" – "Hold Fast".

But the trip had another purpose, and its most interesting aspects were the ones Hemingway did not include: he spent much of the trip "praying and weeping" over his divorce from Hadley, and at one stage stopped at a roadside shrine near La Spezia to atone for the end of his marriage, returning to the car with tears in his eyes. That he should have prayed at a roadside shrine was a sign of an aspect of his life in Italy which he rarely discussed: it had – supposedly – made him a Roman Catholic.

13

A Grand Religion

"'I'm going to sleep' Bill said. He put a newspaper over his face.
'Listen, Jake' he said, 'are you really a Catholic?' 'Technically'.
'What does that mean?' 'I don't know'"

The Sun Also Rises

THE MOST SIGNIFICANT ENCOUNTER of Hemingway's return
to Italy in 1927 was not one of his brushes with Fascist offi-
cialdom, or with restaurant owners and prostitutes, but his reunion
with a priest: Don Giuseppe Bianchi, the Florentine army chaplain
who Hemingway claimed had "baptised" him nearly a decade earlier
while he was lying in the field hospital near Treviso after being
wounded at the Piave front.

This reunion was not by chance. On the contrary, it was the
real point of the 1927 Italian journey, at least for Hemingway. For
Pauline was a Catholic, and to marry Pauline in a Roman Catholic
church he needed to prove that by being given extreme unction at
the frontline he had in effect been baptised into the Roman Catholic faith. He – and Pauline – evidently hoped that Don Giuseppe
would provide a statement to this effect.

Hemingway's religious life until this point – insofar as he had
one – had been entirely Protestant. He had gone to Roman Catholic

churches in Paris while Pauline prayed, Hemingway later told AE Hotchner, but his only connection to Catholicism was his love of images of the crucified Jesus such as Mantegna's masterpiece of perspective *Dead Christ*, also known as *The Lamentation of Christ*, which shows the Virgin Mary and St John weeping over the supine body of Jesus.

Hemingway's mother Grace was a devout Episcopalian, and he was christened at the Oak Park Third Congregational Church on 1 October 1899, his parents' third wedding anniversary. While working for the *Kansas City Star* in 1918 he told his mother that although he did not "rave about religion" he was "as sincere a Christian as I can be". If he failed to attend church on a Sunday it was because he had been up till the early hours helping to get the Sunday edition of the paper out.

"Don't worry or cry or fret about my not being a good Christian. I am just as much as ever and pray every night and believe just as hard so cheer up!" he told her. On the way to the front in Italy the following year, he again wrote to his mother to assure her that he believed in God and Jesus Christ, and had "hopes for a hereafter". His marriage to Hadley took place at the Methodist church at Horton Bay in Michigan, and their son John was christened at St Luke's Episcopal Chapel in Paris.

But Pauline was from a Roman Catholic family: her mother Mary, the daughter of an Irish Catholic, was so devout that her initial reaction when told of her daughter's involvement with Hemingway was to insist on the sanctity of his marriage to Hadley, though she later accepted that their divorce was inevitable. For all the superficial glamour of her life as a *Vogue* reporter in Paris, Pauline too was religious, telling Hemingway she prayed every night to St Joseph to give her "a good, kind, attractive Catholic husband".

What she wanted, Pauline now wrote in one of the letters she sent to Hemingway during the Italian trip, was "conclusive proof" of his baptism so that they could have a Roman Catholic wedding. "Maybe you could find the priest who baptized you", she wrote, unaware – or so it would seem – that Hemingway had already thought of this and was on the case.

A brief mention by Hemingway in a recently discovered letter appears to indicate that his encounter with Don Giuseppe Bianchi took place in the tiny republic of San Marino. "Been up at the Republic of San Marino seeing a priest I knew during the war", Hemingway wrote on Wednesday 23 March to Isidor Schneider, the New York poet and editor. But the "priest I knew during the war" was almost certainly not Don Giuseppe Bianchi but another Don Giuseppe, Don Giuseppe Guidi, who had been the wartime chaplain serving with the San Marino volunteers who ran the field hospital to which Hemingway was taken when he was wounded in 1918, the Villa Toso at Casier.

Guy Hickok had been particularly keen to see San Marino, and so too was Hemingway – not to meet a priest however, but to thank the San Marino doctor who had picked "180 pieces of shell" out of his body at the Villa Toso field hospital (or at least some of them) – the kind of act, Hemingway said, which made for "lasting acquaintances". When they got to San Marino, they learned that the doctor (probably Dr Amadeo Kraus) had moved away. But they found the pharmacist who had served in the field hospital, Luigi Balsimelli, who Hemingway no doubt wanted to thank for saving him from septicemia and gangrene at the Villa Toso.

They evidently also called on another of Hemingway's San Marino acquaintances, a man who had served as an Italian army officer during the war – despite the Republic's neutral stance – and had since risen to be San Marino's most powerful figure: Giuliano Gozi. "Visited San Marino today", Hemingway wrote on a postcard to Ezra Pound from Rimini on Tuesday 22 March, adding that he had had tea with the "minister of foreign affairs".

Some scholars have taken this to be a facetious reference to Mussolini, who at the time combined the foreign affairs portfolio with his role as Duce. It is almost certainly however an allusion not to the Italian dictator but to San Marino-born Gozi, who during the war had fought with Italian Alpini troops on the Austrian front with the rank of lieutenant, and when wounded had been treated by the San Marino hospital volunteers. After the war Gozi rose swiftly to become the tiny Republic's secretary of state for foreign affairs, head of the San Marino Fascist Party and eventually captain-regent, or head of state.

During their tour of San Marino, according to Hickok, they were approached by a "small, thin" priest calling out "Tenente!" ("Lieutenant!") to Hemingway. The priest showed Hemingway and Hickok the high stone towers of San Marino's fortress, commanding a view across the Adriatic to Yugoslavia, and in the town museum pointed out a "chunk" of the Austrian shell which had struck their field hospital at the front and had been brought back as a souvenir. Asked if he remembered this, Hemingway replied, "That was the day everybody who could got under the beds. My leg was in a big cast and I couldn't get under the bed. I guess I remember."

Don Bianchi may have retained his links to the San Marino volunteers, but would not have shown Hemingway and Hickok round the hilltop Republic with the pride of a local cleric. For he was by now not a parish priest but a monk at the Benedictine Olivetan monastery of San Prospero, in the fishing village of Camogli, five kilometres along the Riviera coast from Rapallo, founded in 1883 (and still welcoming guests today).

Don Giuseppe had joined the community of San Prospero after the war, taking the name Brother Gerardo Maria, and by the time of Hemingway's 1927 visit to Italy had been its head for two years (he was made Prior on 30 June 1925). He died in June 1965, was buried at the order's main monastery of Monte Oliveto Maggiore in the countryside near Siena, and always refused to discuss his role in Hemingway's life beyond saying that the writer had been "a very good man".

The encounter between Hemingway and the priest who had "anointed" him almost certainly took place not at San Marino, nor at Rapallo (as some biographers have suggested) but at Camogli, while Hemingway and Hickok were visiting the Pounds. If Don Giuseppe did provide "conclusive proof" in written form, it has never come to light however. It has in any case never been clear what action Don Giuseppe did take in 1918: most probably he gave the last rites, or "extreme unction", to all dying soldiers, a ceremony which Hemingway was able to construe as baptism.

Born in the Florentine suburb of Solliciano, Don Giuseppe first became hospital chaplain at Sarzana, just inland from La Spezia on the main railway line to Pisa. When the First World War broke out he was made chaplain to the 70th Infantry Regiment, the 'Ancona' – hence his presence on the frontline when Hemingway was wounded. Arguably he not only "made Hemingway a Catholic", he saved his life, since it was the priest who found him lying among the war dead and drew the attention of the doctors to the fact that he was still breathing.

The priest would become a character in *A Farewell to Arms*. In the novel Frederic Henry recalls that the chaplain was "young and blushed easily and wore a uniform like the rest of us but with a cross in dark red velvet above the left breast pocket of his gray tunic". The real-life Don Giuseppe was from Florence: the fictional priest comes from Abruzzo, a detail Hemingway took from another of the frontline priests, Don Giovanni Minozzi, the founder of the soldiers' refuges. In a lapse of memory Hemingway later confused the two, telling Hotchner that to marry Pauline he had to "try to convince the church elders that when I had been wounded in Italy and transported to a dressing station, where I was lined up with other wounded, a priest from the Abruzzi anointed us while walking along the row of beds".

In the 1957 film version of *A Farewell to Arms* the priest – who is not named – is played with panache and an ironic smile by a famous and much-loved Italian actor, Alberto Sordi. In the novel the priest is often mocked by the officers in the mess, who tease him for not joining them to enjoy the girls at the local brothel and accuse the Pope and the Vatican of backing the Austrian side in the war. But the priest befriends Frederic – Hemingway's alter ego – and invites him to come and visit his family at Capracotta in the mountains of Abruzzo (now in Molise).

They later discuss the case of Archbishop John Ireland (who died in 1918), a former army chaplain who became Archbishop of St Paul, Minnesota and a controversial social reformer – though Frederic feigns more knowledge of the case than he actually has, confining his contributions to, "Yes father. That is true, father. Perhaps, father. No father, well maybe yes, father. You know more about it than I do, father."

When he heads for the front, Catherine gives him a St Anthony pendant on a gold chain to wear as protection, even though she is not a Catholic. After he is wounded he finds it is missing ("Someone probably got it at one of the dressing stations"). In real life it was in fact Hemingway who had given Agnes a St Anthony pendant, not the other way round. He had no doubt seen, or even prayed at, the shrine to St Anthony which stood at a crossroads at Fossalta, which miraculously survived the shelling which destroyed so much else, and which – although it has since been moved – still offers roadside comfort and reassurance to local Italians.

14

Extreme Unction

"Pauline was worth a Mass"

Patrick Hemingway

THE QUESTION REMAINS: how much of a Catholic was Hemingway? According to AE Hotchner, Hemingway told him his task in going to Italy in 1927 was to "prove I was what I wasn't". In *A Farewell to Arms* the priest visits Frederic at the field hospital bearing gifts – mosquito netting, a bottle of vermouth (which they share) and the English newspapers, which he has bought in Mestre. The talk turns to the war, and to faith: asked if he loves God, Frederic replies that he is "afraid of him in the night sometimes", but cannot love anyone. "You do", the priest answers, reminding him however that passion and lust for women are not the same as love in the sense of "sacrifice and service".

They do not pray together, let alone take Communion, though the priest obviously would like to ("'You do not want me for anything?', he asked hopefully"). In the real rather than fictional world however, Hemingway had come to regard the blessing or anointing he received at the hands of Don Giuseppe while lying seriously wounded as his formal entry into the Roman Catholic Church. He said in 1926 that he had been given "extreme unction" at the front, that Catholicism was "the most comfortable religion for anyone soldiering" and that while there was a lot of "nonsense" in Catholic doctrine he "could not imagine taking any other religion seriously".

He spelled Catholicism with a lower case 'c', but clearly meant Roman Catholic rather than "catholic" in the broader, Anglican sense. There was, he wrote to Ernest Walsh on 2 January 1926, a lot of "rot" in Catholicism, such as "Holy Years etc", and he was not what was called a "good" Catholic. But "if anything I am a catholic. Had extreme unction administered to me as such in July 1918 and recovered. So guess I'm a super-catholic." Shortly afterwards he raised the issue of sainthood with Walsh, saying "Although I am catholic have never had much admiration for martyrs or saints."

According to his son Patrick, who wrote an introduction to the restored version of *A Moveable Feast*, "When my father was free to marry my mother, Pauline, he agreed to convert to Roman Catholicism and undergo a course of religious instruction in Paris. Hemingway, of course, as a boy had received quite a bit of religious instruction as a properly brought-up Protestant, but he had received the sacrament of last rites from a Catholic chaplain in the battlefield dressing station during the night after his mortar wound on the Italian front, and like the famous French king whose statue he mentions in the Paris memoir, he knew that Pauline was worth a Mass."

Not long after the trip to Italy with Hickok, Hemingway admitted to Father Vincent Donovan, a Dominican priest in New York who had questioned him about his faith, that he had not been a good Catholic after his 'baptism' by Don Giuseppe during the war. He had failed to attend Communion regularly, he wrote, but had gone to Mass often in the course of 1926 and had finally "put my house in order" in 1927 after meeting Don Giuseppe again. He was, he said, a "very dumb Catholic" who was trying to lead "a good life". "I have been a Catholic for many years", he told Father Donovan. Hemingway claimed he had not publicised his faith because he did not wish to be seen as "a Catholic writer", not least because he could not claim to have "set a good example".

Much later, in the 1950s, he was visited at his home in Cuba by an American academic, Fraser Drew, who asked if he was a Catholic. "I like to think that I am, insofar as I can be", Hemingway replied. "I can still go to Mass, although many things have happened about divorces and remarriages." He told Drew that a Basque priest he had got to know in Spain prayed for him every day, "as I do for him. I can't pray for myself any more. Perhaps it is because in some way I have become hardened."

This is reminiscent of Frederic Henry in *A Farewell to Arms*, who when asked by Count Greffi if he is a believer replies that he is – "at night". In *The Sun Also Rises* Jake Barnes – yet another alter ego – claims he is "pretty religious": he regrets that he has been "such a rotten Catholic" but says there was nothing he could do about it, "at least for a while, and maybe never", adding that "anyway it was a grand religion and I only wished I felt religious and maybe I would next time".

Jake prays in the cathedral at Pamplona – "It was dim and dark and the pillars went high up, and there were people praying, and it smelt of incense, and there were some wonderful big windows" – but the prayers are for himself, his friends, bullfighting, fishing, a good fiesta and making money, so that he feels ashamed after "kneeling with my forehead on the wood in front of me". Hemingway certainly claimed he went to church regularly while in Spain: "Having been to mass this morning I am now due at the bull fight this afternoon", he wrote to his father from Madrid in May 1926, adding "Wish you were along" (though whether he meant for mass or the bull fight – or both – is not clear).

When he moved from Havana to Idaho at the end of his life, Hemingway could be seen crossing himself every time the news bulletins on the car radio mentioned the impending death of Pope

Pius XII. One of his visitors in Idaho was the actor Gary Cooper, the star of the 1932 film version of *A Farewell to Arms*, who told Hemingway he had converted to Catholicism at his wife's urging. Hemingway replied that he had done the same thing, adding that he still "believed in belief".

For Jeffrey Meyers, Hemingway's Catholicism was his way of distancing himself from – and even "expressing contempt for" – his family's Protestantism and the moral values of Oak Park. It was also "a means of identifying himself with the Latin ritual, customs and culture of Italy, France and Spain" and nourishing the "medieval superstition" he had developed in place of religion, as well as being "a convenient accommodation which pleased Pauline". His friend AE Hotchner was blunter, once declaring that while Pauline was a devout Catholic, Hemingway was "a devout nothing".

According to Hotchner, Hemingway once told him that after marrying Pauline he had suffered a period of impotence, and at Pauline's urging he had got down on his knees and prayed for potency. After getting back into bed they had made love "as if they invented it". "That is why I became a Catholic", Hemingway told Hotchner. Hemingway's son Gregory said his father believed in Catholicism "the way he believed in a glass of whisky on a cold day".

In his book *Hemingway's Dark Night* however, Matthew Nickel argues that Hemingway was much more than a "nominal Catholic": over a period of forty years he attended Mass regularly, celebrated saint's days, and donated thousands of dollars to Catholic churches in Key West and Idaho. He was uncomfortable with the Spanish Church's support for the Fascist side in the Spanish Civil War. It was not very Catholic or Christian "to kill the wounded in the hospital in Toledo with hand grenades or to bomb the working quarter of Madrid for no military reason except to kill poor people", he wrote to fellow novelist Harry Sylvester in February 1937. Priests and bishops had also been killed in Spain, Hemingway acknowledged, but he could not understand why the church was "on the side of the oppressors instead of for the people".

There can be little doubt that facing death when he was struck by an Austrian mortar at the front in July 1918 gave him a private revelation of faith *in extremis*. In a fragment published in the collection *In Our Time* he – or the unnamed narrator – calls on "sweet Jesus" for help during a bombardment at Fossalta: "Dear Jesus please get me out. Christ please please please Christ. If you'll only keep me from getting killed I'll do anything you say. I believe in you and I'll tell every one in the world that you are the only one that matters. Please please dear Jesus. The shelling moved further up the line ... The next night back at Mestre he did not tell the girl he went upstairs with at the Villa Rossa about Jesus. And he never told anybody."

Hemingway was furious when in 1949 Cardinal Francis Spellman of New York – a supporter of Senator Joseph McCarthy, whom Hemingway despised – recruited seminarians to break a strike by "Communist" gravediggers in Queens. Hemingway wrote – though apparently did not send – a scathing letter to the cardinal from Havana accusing him of "arrogance, indolence and fatness", and ending "You will never be Pope as long as I am alive."

Yet he still had Masses said for friends and family, ate fish on Fridays and "visited and revisited important pilgrimage sites and cathedrals". In Paris, Nickel suggests, Hemingway was also profoundly influenced by the "equally idiosyncratic Catholicism" of the poet Baudelaire, and his own fiction is imbued with a sense of original sin and repentance. When torn between Hadley and Pauline he found comfort in Paris in the church of Saint-Sulpice in the Luxembourg Quarter, he later told Hotchner – "twin towers, three tiers of elegant columns, massively delicate" – which had a faded inscription over the entrance celebrating the immortality of the soul, in which he "devoutly believed".

Hemingway's suicide in Idaho in 1961 raised difficult issues for the Catholic Church (as did his four marriages). The compromise solution was a brief funeral service rather than a Mass, held not in the church but at the graveside, with three Ave Marias and three Paternosters. Gianfranco Ivancich, learning of Hemingway's suicide from *Il Gazzettino*, the Venice paper, immediately flew without baggage to Sun Valley via London, Los Angeles and Salt Lake City, sleeping still fully clothed on Hemingway's bed, where he felt "as if the spirit or soul of Ernest was physically, bodily present".

According to Pauline's biographer Ruth Hawkins, although Hemingway had "embraced Catholicism when it suited him", he "showed his true feelings when he blamed the breakup of his marriage to Pauline on the church", claiming that it was Pauline's insistence on practising *coitus interruptus* because of the Church's stance on birth control which had pushed him into the arms of Martha Gellhorn, his third wife. Pauline evidently thought so too, telling Mary Welsh, Hemingway's fourth wife (the two got on surprisingly well), "If I hadn't been such a bloody fool practicing Catholic, I wouldn't have lost my husband." In her memoir *How It Was* Mary suggests this was a reference to birth control, adding "I wondered but never asked and never heard."

Whatever proof Don Giuseppe did or did not provide for them in 1927, Hemingway and Pauline were married in Paris on 10 May at the Roman Catholic Church of St Honore d'Eylau, following a civil ceremony in the town hall of the 14th arrondissement. He took a course of instruction with local Catholic clergy beforehand, no doubt assuring them that his conversion during the war had been sincere. Pauline's parents did not travel to Paris for the wedding. But Mary Pfeiffer evidently reconciled herself to the match – and to Hemingway: "For many months I have been asking Our Heavenly Father to make the crooked ways straight and your life's pathway one of peace and happiness, and this morning I feel a quiet assurance that my prayers have not been in vain", she wrote to him after the Paris ceremony.

The following year he started to write *A Farewell to Arms*, at first called *In Another Country*, a quotation from Christopher Marlowe: "But that was in another country, and besides the wench is dead." Instead he used that title for his Nick Adams story, and turned to the Oxford Book of English Verse for his tale of the doomed love affair of Frederic and Catherine, settling on George Peele's poem. Frederic Henry is not overtly Christian, but then he is not an atheist either: as Catherine lies dying in childbirth he begs God not to let her die.

But then *A Farewell to Arms* was a form of catharsis, a working through – together with the Nick Adams stories – of all his Italian dramas, spiritual, physical and emotional. After his encounter with Don Giuseppe in 1927 and his marriage to Pauline, Hemingway turned his back on Italy. He did not return for twenty years. When he did, it was not Milan or Sicily he took to his heart: it was Venice.

15

Harry's Bar

"Every time I hear someone say Hemingway sure gave you a lot of free promotion, I say it was me and my bar that promoted *him*"

Giuseppe Cipriani

ERNEST HEMINGWAY and his wife docked at Genoa in the Polish steamer *Jagiello*, had his Buick Roadmaster convertible unloaded, hired a chauffeur called Riccardo and set off for Stresa. He was back. The year was 1948, and Hemingway's wife this time was Mary Welsh – his fourth and last. "Christ, this is a wonderful country", Hemingway wrote to his friend Colonel Charles Trueman Lanham (known as Buck), a US army officer he had become close to while covering the battles in Normandy during the Second World War.

Hemingway was no longer the strapping youngster who had been wounded on the frontline in 1918, had fallen in love with his nurse but had then married Hadley, taking her to Italy in the 1920s to show her the haunts of his youth. Hemingway – now universally known as Papa – was here fifty years old, bulkier, portlier and certainly drinking too much, as he did throughout his life. But he was now famous, and looking for inspiration for his next novel – in Italy.

It had been a busy twenty years. In 1928 Hemingway and his

second wife Pauline had moved from Paris to Key West in Florida, and Pauline gave birth successively to two sons, Patrick and Gregory, with difficult labours in both cases. Hemingway's father Ed, dogged by worries over finances and poor health, had shot himself that same year with the pistol his father Anson had carried during the American Civil War. Hemingway became estranged from his mother, who he resented as domineering. His relations with Pauline became strained and he had affairs, notably with Jane Mason, a married woman, while ostensibly on fishing expeditions to Cuba and Bimini.

But he became a celebrity. Hemingway's fame as a writer began with *A Farewell to Arms* in 1929 and *Death in the Afternoon* in 1933. The 1930s took him to Spain and to Africa for safaris in the Serengeti, the latter producing *Green Hills of Africa*, and his experiences as a reporter in the Spanish Civil War inspiring *For Whom the Bell Tolls*, perhaps his finest novel. In Spain he also helped to produce a film about the anti-Franco struggle, *The Spanish Earth*, raising $20,000 in Hollywood for the Republican cause.

Spain brought Hemingway closer to the war correspondent Martha Gellhorn, who he had first met at Key West when she walked into Sloppy Joe's bar and found Hemingway drinking there (as he often did), a large man "in untidy, somewhat soiled white shorts and shirt". In a replay of Pauline's behaviour in forming a *menage a trois* with Hemingway and Hadley, Martha became a fixture in the Key West home, becoming Hemingway's third wife in 1940.

The new couple set up house in Cuba (which Hemingway already knew well from his fishing trips from Florida), renting and then buying Finca Vigia (Lookout Farm), a Spanish colonial farmstead twelve miles from Havana. Together they also discovered Sun Valley in Idaho as a holiday getaway, where in the 1950s Hemingway would get to know the actor Gary Cooper, star of the film version of *For Whom the Bell Tolls*.

This was the shortest of his marriages however, and the

Hemingway-Gellhorn union fell apart under the strain of professional rivalry as competing reporters during the Second World War. Hemingway flew on bombing missions with the RAF, but never forgave Martha for the fact that although both took part in the D-Day landings as war correspondents, she managed to get ashore with the troops while he stayed on a hospital ship (though he did later witness the Allied liberation of Normandy and Paris).

There was also Martha's growing irritation – as Carlos Baker puts it – with the fact that Hemingway's "egotism often carried him far beyond the call of genius", as well as with his tendency for "self-dramatisation" and his conviction that "life was stale and weary without manufactured glamour". During the war in France and the Rhineland, he was accused of often going far beyond his role as a reporter and acting as a combatant, taking command of troops, keeping bazookas and other weapons in his room and at one point throwing grenades into a cellar where SS officers were thought to be hiding.

In 1946 Martha gave way to Mary Welsh, a petite, married *Time* magazine writer in her thirties whom Hemingway had met in wartime London and again in liberated Paris, where he had taken a room at the Ritz. Mary must have had doubts, not least when Hemingway placed a photograph of her husband, Noel Monks, an Australian reporter for the *Daily Mail*, on a toilet bowl at the Ritz and fired at it with a pistol.

Hemingway claimed he had personally 'liberated' Paris – though in reality he only 'liberated' the bar at the Ritz, distributing (and drinking) quantities of champagne. Nonetheless Mary divorced Monks (they had drifted apart in the war) and married Hemingway in Havana. Bizarrely she and two of the other Mrs Hemingways, Hadley and Pauline, all got on well with each other – Pauline at one point even came to live with Hemingway and Mary in Cuba.

But Italy beckoned. Hemingway's memory of his 1918 Red Cross experiences had stayed with him all his life. While in Cuba he had written the preface to an anthology called *Men at War*, recalling his trauma, but then observing that "nothing could happen to me that had not happened to all men before me". It was here that he recorded how the Fossalta di Piave experience had destroyed all "illusion of immortality" for him.

Now he resolved to show Mary, who had never visited the country, the scene of his early brush with death, just as he had shown it to Hadley over twenty years before. If he remembered the disappointment of that trip, he did not share it with Mary, who was enchanted by Italy as they set off in the Buick – royal blue with bright red lining and seats.

Hemingway had at first suggested a break in Provence after admiring a book of Cezanne reproductions. "Why not?" Mary had replied. "Let's take the Buick. And hire a chauffeur there, so you can look instead of always driving." Mary (who thought her husband enjoyed martinis rather too much to drive safely) had noticed a smartly painted Polish ship, the *Jagiello*, which plied from Havana to Genoa via Cannes with an Italian crew and which – "maybe" – could have a car lashed to its forward deck.

And so in September 1948 the Hemingways set off, enjoying stops on the way at Madeira and Lisbon. They had intended to disembark at Cannes for the tour of Provence, but there was a storm, and so they sailed on instead to Genoa, where the warm welcome, the shouts of "*che bella macchina*" ("what a beautiful car!") and the sound of "friendly sing song" Italian so entranced Hemingway that he decided to return to Stresa and Lake Maggiore and forget about Provence altogether.

They headed first to Milan, where the publisher Alberto Mondadori told Hemingway he was the most widely read author in Italy, "from common sailors to the nobility". He had his Italian royalties deposited in a Milan bank to finance his future trips. They then drove (or rather Riccardo drove) to Stresa, where the hotel doorman, to Mary's astonishment, emerged after a gap of several decades to greet them with "Welcome back, Signor Hemingway". The tour continued to Como and Bergamo, and then up to Cortina d'Ampezzo, which was much as it had been in 1923 when Hemingway, Hadley and Renata Borgatti had spent the winter there enjoying the fine dining and stunning mountain views.

This time he and Mary stayed not at the Hotel Bellevue but at the equally grand Hotel Concordia, which was officially closed for the autumn but offered to open up just for Hemingway and Mary. Hemingway – apparently forgetting his visits in the 1920s, or choosing to forget them – said he was enjoying the chance to "rediscover" Northern Italy, which he had previously seen only from crowded military trucks or through the dust goggles he had worn while driving his Fiat ambulance.

He now met his Italian translator, Fernanda Pivano, who had been arrested during the Second World War for translating *A Farewell to Arms*, which the Mussolini regime considered a "defeatist" work. She later said Hemingway had sent her a postcard reading "I'm in Cortina and I would like to meet you", but she threw it away, thinking it was a joke in poor taste. It was only when Hemingway wrote to her again, saying he would come to Turin (her home town) if she did not come to Cortina, that she realised he really was there and really did want to see her. He wrote to her after their first meeting that she was pretty but also had a good brain, signing himself "Mr Papa".

He also met Fernanda's soon-to-be husband, the noted architect Ettore Sottsass, who would later become an internationally recognised designer for Olivetti, among others. Fernanda and Ettore (who was born in Innsbruck) took Hemingway and Mary on a local tour by car of the Austrian border, past the spectacular Three Peaks of Lavaredo high in the Dolomites to Toblach (Dobbiaco), not far from Bolzano.

They stopped to eat in the town of Bruneck (Brunico) in the Puster Valley, where Mary bought local ceramics, and returned to Cortina late at night via the Campolungo Pass and the ski resort of Arabba. Fernanda's memories of the trip included a scolding from Hemingway over her refusal to drink: he was convinced that not drinking was "a wretched vice". "To tell the truth, I was a little bit convinced of it too."

At Cortina Hemingway got up early, breakfasting on caffe latte and crisp freshly baked bread with lashings of butter before heading for the bar at the Hotel Posta or La Genzianella cafe. As usual he was taken up by local aristocrats, in this case Count Federico Kechler and his wife Maria Luisa. Hemingway went trout fishing at their private reserve in the Anterselva Valley (or Antholzertal) of South Tyrol high in the Dolomites, and also met Federico's brothers Alberto and Carlo at other Kechler estates, Fraforeano and San Martino di Codroipo in nearby Friuli. At the Kechler villa at Fraforeano the guest book still has Hemingway's inscription thanking Alberto and his wife Costanza "for a lovely visit and a good shoot" on 24 October 1948, to which Mary added in French "et sa femme Mary".

Hemingway, sometimes accused of cultivating aristocrats, had in this case at least not gone out of his way to seek high society – he had simply asked Luigi Zambelli, the owner of a local sports equipment shop, for advice on trout fishing, and had been put in touch with Federico Kechler. They met up in the bar of the Hotel Posta, and got on famously, with Kechler speaking English with "a pure Mayfair accent". "I think it was simply that Hemingway found in our families people with the means to provide him with hunting and fishing", Alberto's daughter Ciccinella Kechler told me at the Fraforeano villa. "It was not snobbery, it was rather that we could help him lead the kind of life he wanted to lead."

In October 1948 Hemingway and Mary decided to rent a house

in Cortina for the winter, choosing the Villa Aprile in the suburb of Donea on the outskirts of the town, with views across gently sloping hills. The rent was paid by Mondadori. Fernanda Pivano, who stayed there, reports that it had a main bedroom, a guest bedroom, a sitting room and a study for Hemingway, who wrote at the villa on his Corona typewriter, a bottle of Valpolicella always on the table. He and Mary ate at a nearby rural trattoria with just two tables in a single room, where his favourite dish was *baccala all veneta* (dried and salted cod Venetian style), cooked in oil and served with polenta.

It was now that Venice entered his life as much as the Veneto had done. From Cortina they drove down through Belluno and Treviso to La Serenissima, which Hemingway found was "absolutely god-damned wonderful", especially for those who cared about history. After all, the Grand Canal, he wrote to Fernanda Pivano, had inspired Byron, Browning and D'Annunzio. Mary too was smitten: she describes in her memoir *How It Was* a city of "exquisite bridges, the moon just after full, coming up grandly over the Grand Canal".

Indeed, Venice and the Veneto have always held a fatal fascination for writers, from Lord Byron and Henry James to Thomas Mann and Oscar Wilde – and now Ernest Hemingway. All of them were enchanted and exhilarated by the lagoon city – yet it also (sometimes later, sometimes at the same moment) aroused in them feelings of sadness and melancholy. As Henry James remarked, Venice has been painted and described so many times that of all the cities of the world it is "the easiest to visit without going there".

Their favourite places during this first post-war trip would become Hemingway's Venetian haunts, notably the Hotel Gritti Palace on the Grand Canal. Housed in a Gothic fifteenth-century palazzo, the Gritti was not the home of the Doge, Andrea Gritti, but was commissioned by him and used by ambassadors to the Venetian Republic from the Holy See in Rome. It later became the property of his descendants, the Gritti family, who bought it from an equally prominent Venetian ducal family, the Pisanis, in the nineteenth century and turned it into a hotel. Previous guests had included John Ruskin, author of the three-volume *The Stones of Venice*, his influential study of Venetian architecture.

The Hemingways, Mary wrote in her diary, were lodged in "a huge inconvenient room just opposite the church of Santa Maria della Salute on the Grand Canal", with a Venetian chandelier. The location was – and is – stunning: following a meticulous restoration of the hotel in 2012–2013, the Hemingways' room on the first floor is now the Hemingway Suite, complete with his favourite club chair and – inevitably – a well-stocked bar. It was, AE Hotchner recalled, "a large room with high, arching windows facing the Grand Canal, beautifully furnished with Venetian antique furniture".

There were few things more pleasant in life, wrote Somerset Maugham, than "to sit on the terrace of the Gritti when the sun about to set bathes in lovely colour the Salute, which almost faces you". From the terrace today you can admire the Salute to your left and the Guggenheim Museum to your right, housed since 1951 in the Palazzo Venier dei Leoni, which Peggy Guggenheim had bought three years earlier to house her art collection.

The terrace of the Gritti now became Hemingway's home from home in Venice. So, too, did Harry's Bar, owned by the Cipriani family; the Rialto fish market; and the Café Florian. As a journalist Mary later wrote a brief history of Harry's Bar, explaining how Giuseppe Cipriani, the barman at the Europa Hotel on the Grand Canal, had lent money to a hard-up American from Boston called Harry Pickering, who in 1931 not only repaid the loan but helped Cipriani establish the chic and cosy bar named after him.

It soon became the haunt of the rich and famous: "When you push open the narrow glass front door, frosted for the privacy of the guests", Mary wrote, "you step up onto a slightly heated floor of Roman travertine marble which is twenty nine feet long, shorter than a gondola, and fourteen feet wide ... Anybody who is anybody – as well as anybodies who aren't anybody – has been a customer at Harry's."

Hemingway was particularly fond of martinis at Harry's Bar. According to Arrigo Cipriani, the son of the founder, the secret lay not only in keeping the bottles in the freezer but also in the 15–1 proportion of gin to vermouth, a cocktail Hemingway took to calling 'Montgomerys', an allusion to his assertion that during the Second World War the British field marshal – the victor of El Alamein – had only taken on the enemy if he could be sure of a 15–1 advantage in troop numbers.

They took a tourist boat trip across the lagoon from the Fondamente Nuove (still the point of departure for lagoon vaporettos today), past Murano, the glass-blowing island, and Burano, the lace island, to lunch at the inn on Torcello, which like Harry's Bar was owned by the Ciprianis. On Torcello he was much taken by the magnificent mosaics at the former Cathedral (or Basilica) of Santa Maria Assunta, especially those depicting the Last Judgement and the Virgin Mary, and by the so-called Throne of Attila, the fifth-century stone which stands in front of the cathedral, and which although it was probably never used by the leader of the Huns certainly dates to the earliest Torcello settlement.

"Venice is more beautiful, and more mixed up, than I could have imagined", Mary told her diary in October 1948. "There is not only the Cafe Florian, rather like Maxim's in Paris, where Casanova used to eat and drink. There are the thirteenth-century mosaics, Byzantine, in St Mark's along with the mosaics copied from modern eighteenth-century painters showing all of Noah's story, the ark and afterwards, also the whole story, in precise lines, of Adam and Eve." There was also the Ducal (Doge's) Palace, and the mellow sound of the bells.

To his delight Hemingway was made a Knight of the Order of Malta (Cavaliere di Gran Croce al Merito), and despite the fact that he had only been a Red Cross ambulance driver up in the Dolomites somehow persuaded himself he had defended Venice itself in his youth by standing chest-deep in the salt marshes of the lagoon at Capo Sile.

But he did also once again revisit the real site of his youthful heroism at Fossalta di Piave, which as on his previous sentimental journey in the 1920s he found had been rebuilt, this time after another world war. The crater where the Austrian mortar had exploded next to him on that now distant night was now covered with grass.

He wanted to defecate symbolically at the spot, but instead settled for digging a hole with a stick and inserting a 1000-lire note to symbolise having left blood and money in Italian soil. He now began to develop the idea of a story which would take as its theme the impact on a man of fifty – himself – both of Venice and of the re-visited scenes of his youthful wartime exploits in the Veneto over thirty years before: *Across The River and Into the Trees*.

16

Adriana and Renata

"I hope you will like this book. Do you know Venice? It is about Venice and it seems very simple unless you know what it is all about. It is really about bitterness, soldiering, honour, love and death"

Hemingway to General Eric Dorman-
O'Gowan ('Chink'), 2 May 1950

HEMINGWAY SPENT THE REST of October at the Locanda Cipriani on Torcello, writing in the morning and duck shooting in the afternoon. He had thought of moving on to Portofino, but settled for Torcello the moment he saw the quarters – a sitting room with a fireplace and French windows overlooking the gardens and the Cathedral, not to mention a bedroom with two big beds and an adjoining yellow bathroom. According to Mary, at Torcello Hemingway told her stories of his boyhood in Oak Park – though "in such precise detail that I could never detect when he skidded off fact into fiction".

Mary went off for a few days to Florence in the Buick (Riccardo again at the wheel) to stay with Alan Moorehead, the Australian-born war correspondent and author, and his wife Lucy (Milner), who had rented the Villa Diana at Fiesole, once the home of the Medici poet Angelo Ambrogini, or Poliziano. The Mooreheads had rented the villa in September 1948, moving in with their children, John and Caroline, later the distinguished author and biographer of Martha Gellhorn.

Moorehead, who admired *A Farewell to Arms* and was attempting to follow in Hemingway's footsteps with action novels such as *The Rage of the Vulture*, had visited the Hemingways at Cortina with Lucy. He found Hemingway "a walking myth of himself", his layers of clothing festooned with duck shooting cartridges and teals and mallards, his beard flecked with snow – though Moorehead also saw the serious and dedicated writer beneath the layers, a man who "writes and re-writes for as long as his brain will work, knowing that it is only by a miracle that he will ever achieve a phrase, or even a word, that will correspond to the vision in his mind".

Nonetheless Hemingway did not accompany Mary to Fiesole, preferring to stay behind in Venice and write. At the Villa Diana the Mooreheads' guests included JB Priestley who – apparently forgetting he had once threatened to sue Mary for a waspish *Time* magazine piece about him – offered to introduce Mary to the art historian and critic Bernard Berenson, now aged 83, at his palatial home in Fiesole, the Villa I Tatti.

Mary found Berenson – in "faultless blue suit, gray fedora and gray suede gloves" – in the garden, introducing herself as Mrs Hemingway. When Berenson asked her "What number?" she was baffled, thinking he perhaps numbered his guests. He explained that he wished to know which number wife she was, and when she answered "number four" Berenson expressed wonder at Hemingway's ability to "get through so many wives".

Mary explained that Ernest was "a man of tremendous energy and exuberance", leading Berenson to ask bluntly whether he "demonstrated these characteristics in bed". They arrived at the villa before she could think of a reply, but "Lucy, noticing my strawberry-red face, giggled knowingly". Hemingway evidently later regretted not having gone to Fiesole with Mary: he much admired Berenson, he wrote to the art connoisseur later, but did not much care for Florence, being "an old Veneto boy myself".

The Hemingways then returned to Cortina, where on a rainy Saturday afternoon in December Hemingway went partridge and duck shooting with Carlo Kechler, Count Federico's brother, and another Veneto aristocrat he had got to know well, Baron Nanuk Franchetti, on the Franchetti estate at San Gaetano near Caorle. And it was here that Hemingway became acquainted with the young woman who would capture his heart: Adriana Ivancich, better known as Renata, the beguiling heroine of *Across the River and Into the Trees*.

Adriana was the only woman present that day at the duck shoot. She was 18, Hemingway 49. She had never been on a shoot before; bedraggled and fed up at being whacked on the head by ejected cartridge cases, she was drying her hair before an open fire in the kitchen of the hunting lodge when Hemingway saw her. When Adriana told him she could do with a comb, Hemingway gave her some whisky to warm her up and broke his own comb in two for her to use, a gesture he came to see as offering a love token.

Adriana was a slender, dark beauty with a narrow, pale face and hazel eyes. Softly spoken, she was always drawing small cartoons and sketches. Adriana had been educated in Switzerland and at a Catholic girls' day school in Venice, and at the time she met Hemingway was still leading a chaperoned life under the eye of her widowed mother, Dora, who Hemingway had met at Cortina in the 1920s, together with Dora's sister-in-law, Emma Ivancich.

Adriana's illustrious and wealthy family had originally come from the island of Lussino (Mali Losinj) off the coast of Dalmatia, now in Croatia but at the time a Venetian possession. The Ivancichs established themselves in Venice itself at the beginning of the 1800s in a sixteenth-century canalside palazzo in the Calle del Rimedio just off the Piazza San Marco, the Palazzo Rota-Ivancich. It is still owned by the family and still has its sixteenth-century Sansovino ceiling decorations and the family crest, but is used for exhibitions and cultural events such as the Venice Biennale.

The Ivancichs also had a magnificent villa and estate at San Michele al Tagliamento, the Villa Mocenigo (or Villa Biaggini) on the Tagliamento River opposite the ancient Roman river port of Latisana. The great villa was designed by Baldassare Longhena, the seventeenth-century architect of the church of Santa Maria della Salute, which Hemingway could see to the left from his window at the Gritti Palace on the other side of the Grand Canal. Originally built at the end of the sixteenth century for the aristocratic Mocenigo family, which provided a series of Venetian Doges, the villa was bought in the nineteenth century by Vincenzo Biaggini, a businessman from Padua who modernised the farm and estate.

It then passed to the Ivancichs when Biaggini's daughter, Elina, married Giacomo Ivancich, Adriana's grandfather. During the First World War the villa was used as an Italian and then an Austro-Hungarian army field hospital, but in the Second World War it was destroyed by American bombers aiming at a nearby bridge. The Ivancich family were left with the chapel and the typically Venetian colonnaded barns and stables (*barchesse*) which were designed – like the villa itself – by Longhena, and which are still preserved, together with the *cantina* or winery.

Just over the Tagliamento River in Friuli was the Kechler estate at San Martino di Codroipo, and almost on the lagoon itself was the Franchetti estate at San Gaetano, near the lagoon port of Caorle. Raimondo Franchetti, a noted Italian explorer, had given his children exotic names – including his son Nanuk, from the Inuit for polar bear. It was a close-knit world of Venetian aristocrats: Gianfranco Ivancich's wife Cristina, herself from a distinguished Cuban family, later married Nanuk Franchetti after she and Gianfranco had separated in the 1960s.

Hemingway also got to know the di Robilants. Carlo di Robilant would become the model for Count Andrea in *Across the River* ("a very tall man with a ravaged face of great breeding"), while Franchetti was Baron Alvarito, a shy man "beautifully built in his town clothes". Their estates now became an essential part of Hemingway's life, as did the Kechlers, the Franchettis, the di Robilants and the Ivancichs – above all Adriana.

It was not a romantic first encounter. Adriana had agreed to meet them at the crossroads at Latisana, close to her home at the Villa Mocenigo. But she was left standing in the rain after Hemingway stayed much too long with Carlo Kechler at Codroipo and then with Alberto Kechler at Fraforeano – also in nearby Friuli – before making the drive to the Franchetti estate. Hemingway apologised, saying to her (in a remark which curiously foreshadowed his novel about her), "I understand you live across the river".

Hemingway, she wrote later in her memoir *La Torre Bianca* (*The White Tower*), was not as old as she first thought, and had a friendly manner and penetrating eyes. She recalled almost giving up as she waited in the rain, crossing over the bridge several times to look in the Latisana shop windows but then returning. When the blue Buick eventually arrived Hemingway apologised – "terribly sorry Adriana, it's all my fault" – and she forgave him. "So this was Hemingway, the man all Venice was talking about".

As they got to know each other better Adriana found him gentle and understanding in manner, "tall and big, sweet and sometimes almost timid". She instinctively understood him, and often finished his sentences for him. He, for his part, was entranced, not to say infatuated – he later wrote to Adriana to say that his son Gregory thought she was the loveliest girl he had ever seen, a sentiment with which Hemingway wholeheartedly agreed.

But he treated Adriana with paternalism, calling her "Daughter", a term of endearment he had begun using toward all young women. It was in his fiction rather than real life that he – or at least Richard Cantwell, yet another of his alter egos – would have a sexual encounter with Adriana, in a gondola, giving her the name 'Renata' – literally 'reborn' in Italian, symbolising the spirit of Venice and the lagoon as well as the innocence, idealism and courage he felt he had lost because of war and the subsequent embitterments of life.

Cantwell meets Renata/Adriana at Harry's Bar in *Across the River*: "Then she came into the room, shining in her youth and tall striding beauty and the carelessness the wind had made of her hair. She had a pale, almost olive-coloured skin, a profile that could break your, or anyone else's, heart, and her dark hair, of an alive texture, hung down over her shoulders." Her musical voice reminds him of Pablo Casals playing the cello. "I had so much life, so much enthusiasm that I transmitted it to him", the real Adriana said later. "He had begun writing again and suddenly everything seemed easy."

For Irina Ivancich, Adriana's niece, there is no doubt that despite the obvious mutual attraction, "Adriana was much more than just an *amica* for Hemingway, she was a literary and artistic figure in her own right." Adriana and her older brother Gianfranco (Irina's father), she says, were "well read, cultured and outward looking – they were people Hemingway could relate to and in whose company he felt comfortable". Hemingway held an undoubted fascination for both Adriana and Gianfranco, but "he was part of the tapestry of the Ivancich family, not the other way round. The Ivancichs were associated with many writers and artists – D'Annunzio, Pound, Marinetti". As Carlos Baker notes in the introduction to Hemingway's *Selected Letters*, in the final decade of his life Hemingway "wrote often to Adriana and Gianfranco Ivancich, the sister and brother who formed the nucleus of what he called the 'Venetian branch' of his family".

On that fateful rainy winter's day on the Franchetti estate Hemingway asked Adriana to meet Mary over lunch: she brought with her her scrapbook, to which Hemingway added his autograph. He and Mary then spent a quiet 1948 Christmas at Cortina, drinking lots of Bloody Marys. He read the English version of Elio Vittorini's anti-Fascist novel *Conversations in Sicily* in galley proof, and wrote an introduction praising the way Vittorini (who modelled his narrative style on Hemingway's) had captured the essence of Sicily, from its "wine, bread, salt and vinegar" to the sea, hills and valleys, porcupines, grouse and "the smell of sweet grass and fresh-smoked leather".

Early in 1949 Mary had a skiing accident, breaking her right anklebone, and a few months later, in March, Ernest suffered both a severe chest cold and an eye infection, *erisypelas*, going to Padua for treatment. He also found time to visit Verona, where he admired the Roman amphitheatre and enjoyed the 12 Apostoli restaurant, founded in the eighteenth century by twelve Verona merchants. The owner, Giorgio Gioco, was surprised to see a "big man in shirt-sleeves" fetching a bottle of Amarone from the cellar but good naturedly cooked him a meal of steak and "risotto all'Amarone" to go with it.

Mary stayed in Venice, where at the Gritti Palace she encountered the novelist Sinclair Lewis, the celebrated author of *Main Street*, *Babbitt* and *Elmer Gantry*, who had won the Nobel Prize for Literature in 1930. Hemingway had first got to know Lewis in his Paris years with Hadley in the 1920s, but disliked both the man and his work.

Lewis informed Mary that although he loved Hemingway, he had not written enough, was a snob, and moreover had never thanked Lewis properly for his praise of *For Whom the Bell Tolls*. Lewis suggested it must be dreadful for Mary to be married to a genius, and left her to pay the bill. "Mary ended up paying for all his drinks", Hemingway told his publisher Charles Scribner in July 1949. "I told the bartender that if he ever showed again to give him a Mickey Finn which he promised to do."

17

Across the River

"Hemingway was not much of a hunter"

Fiorindo Silotto, 1950s boatman at San Gaetano

THE EYE INFECTION and treatment in Padua had interrupted Hemingway's befriending of Adriana. But on his return from hospital in Padua Hemingway had lunch at the Gritti with both her and her older brother Gianfranco, 28, who had fought in an Italian tank regiment at the battle of El Alamein but had joined the OSS (the forerunner of the CIA) and become an anti-Nazi partisan in the Veneto. Gianfranco would enjoy Hemingway's company, Adriana assured her brother, adding "He is truly intelligent, and he amuses me."

The two men did indeed hit it off at once. Gianfranco, who was evacuated from Africa by the Red Cross, had been wounded in the leg, just as Hemingway himself had been in the First World War – a coincidence, Gianfranco says in his memoir, which made them "comrades in arms".

After the war Gianfranco had returned to the family estate at San Michele al Tagliamento, the Villa Mocenigo, to find not only that it had been bombed by mistake by American warplanes but also that his and Adriana's father, Count Carlo Ivancich, had been murdered in an alleyway in the town during the chaos of war. One theory is that he was killed by local criminals who had stolen provisions and money Carlo had given to partisans fighting the Fascists – though the family is convinced he was a victim of infighting among the partisans themselves, with Communist partisans targeting him for supporting their more democratic rivals.

Hemingway helped Gianfranco both financially and with his career. The younger man, by coincidence, had been offered a job with the Venetian Sidarma shipping agency in Cuba, and was amazed to find that Hemingway lived there. "I had not the faintest idea that the celebrated author had a house at Havana", he writes in his memoir. "In fact I knew very little about him, though I had read his books." Hemingway invited Gianfranco to Cuba, and eventually helped him to buy a farm there. It was behaviour which showed the generous side of his character – but was clearly also a way of staying close to Adriana.

Hemingway became something of a regular at the Franchetti estate. Giovanni Simoncin, who carved decoy ducks to entice real ducks for hunters to shoot, once recalled the day when Baron Franchetti came to his house at Trepalade with a tall, bearded man and introduced him as "my friend Ernest". "But I already know your mother", Hemingway told Simoncin, explaining that he was writing at Torcello, where Simoncin's mother, a lace embroiderer, also sold Torcello souvenirs. "They often used to hunt in the Baron's estate at San Gaetano near Caorle", Simoncin told local historian Camillo Pavan.

He also hunted hares and pheasants at the eighteenth-century villa and riverside estate of Alberto Kechler (known as Titi) in the medieval village of Fraforeano, where Alberto's daughters Ciccinella and Donatella told me they remember the flagon of red wine which staff were instructed to leave outside Hemingway's bedroom door, and which was invariably empty by the morning.

Hemingway was in reality "too passionate as a hunter", according to Baron Alberto Franchetti, Nanuk's son, who as a boy was often present when Hemingway went duck hunting on the Franchetti estate at San Gaetano. "Most of the hunters would bag at least thirty or forty birds, and I myself would shoot perhaps a dozen or more, but Hemingway only ever shot a handful – though he was very proud of the few he had." Hemingway also cut an odd shambling figure, Franchetti recalls, a "huge man" in Canadian flying boots open at the top, military trousers and "a green jacket of the kind the hippies wore later".

Hunting was an all-male affair, usually at the weekends, with the gentlemen of the party – who unlike Hemingway all wore ties and smart Loden jackets – backed up by ghillies, known in Italian simply as 'the men' (*uomini*), one for each guest. The 'men' carried the hunters' guns, cartridges and bags. The lagoon or *valle* had a wooden observation tower, or *altana*, from which the party could assess the situation: windy and rainy days were preferable because they drove wildfowl in from the coast.

As the estate owner, Baron Nanuk Franchetti would consult his head ghillie (*capocaccia*, or *capovalle*) when to start shooting – and in which order. The party assembled in the afternoon on the Saturday, and ate supper in a brick lodge (*casone*) with a fireplace in the long dining room downstairs and rooms upstairs, equipped with fireplaces and oil lamps but no electricity or heating. Hemingway was especially fond of grilled eel, including the skin.

The hunters then played cards until midnight, when they settled down to sleep for a few hours before being woken around 4 am on Sunday morning to start hunting. Hemingway was often unable to sleep however, Franchetti recalls. "He would write in his notebook, standing up, or walk up and down in the dark and then go into the ghillies' huts and wake them up to ask in the mixture of English, French, Italian and Spanish which he called his Lingua

Franca about the weather outlook for the shoot, or where ducks slept at night."

At dawn Nanuk Franchetti would decide which positions the guests could take for the shoot instead of drawing lots (as was traditional), invariably assigning the closest spots to Hemingway so that he could reach them easily with the help of his boatman (*barcaiolo*). The sound of a hunting horn signalled the end of the shoot, Alberto Franchetti recalls, "but Hemingway was always the last one back, his game bag and the crate of gin he took with him both nearly empty".

Yet Hemingway's descriptions of hunting in *Across the River and Into the Trees*, Franchetti acknowledges, are "masterly": he describes a hunter (dressed in "hip boots and an old combat jacket") setting off two hours before daylight with a boatman down the icy canal with his guns and wooden decoys to the lagoon hides, or "pit blinds" made of sunken oak barrels, or *botte*. "From behind him, he heard the incoming whisper of wings and he crouched, took hold of his right-hand gun with his right hand as he looked up from under the rim of the barrel, then stood to shoot at the two ducks that were dropping down, their wings set to brake, coming down dark in the grey dim sky, slanting towards the decoys."

As David Wyatt has noted in *The Hemingway Review* (Spring 2016), the opening of the novel is "so hauntingly beautiful that a reader can be sad to leave it". "They started two hours before daylight", Hemingway begins, "and at first, it was not necessary to break the ice across the canal as other boats had gone on ahead". Each boat has a boatman (or 'poler') standing in the stern, invisible in the dark, the shooter on a stool fastened to a box containing his shells and his lunch, guns propped up against wooden decoys, and "a dog who shifted and shivered uneasily at the sound of the wings of the ducks that passed overhead in the darkness".

What began as a short story about duck shooting in the lagoon however swiftly developed into something much more ambitious:

the story of a 50-year-old man (himself) revisiting the landscape where he had been wounded as a boy of 18 on the Basso Piave within "distant eyeshot" of Venice. *Across the River and Into the Trees* was still only a sketch when Hemingway and Mary boarded the *Jagiello* at Genoa at the end of April 1949 for their return journey to Havana. But it grew into a novel, with Adriana as its focus.

The book's title is taken from the dying words of Thomas 'Stonewall' Jackson, the Confederate General in the American Civil War: "Let us cross over the river and rest under the shade of the trees." It begins with 50-year-old Cantwell looking back over his life while duck hunting "down in the marshes at the mouth of the Tagliamento". Cantwell is clearly Hemingway, though the character also draws on his army friends Major General 'Buck' Lanham, and 'Chink' Dorman-Smith.

Cantwell has come to Venice in his Buick from Trieste, where two days earlier he had undergone a check-up for heart disease. His driver, a mechanic from Wyoming, is called Jackson (presumably a nod to the Civil War general who provided the novel's title). Cantwell is on medication but is told he is in "good shape", apart from a relic of his wartime wounds, a "slightly misshapen" hand which had been "shot through twice".

The journey to Venice takes him "along the old road that ran from Montfalcone to Latisana", a landscape which reminds Cantwell of the First World War when – like Hemingway himself – he had been wounded. It "moved him as it had when he was eighteen years old and had seen it first, understanding nothing of it and only knowing that it was beautiful". But it all looks different now: "Everything is much smaller when you are older."

They pass a bridge and a villa destroyed in the more recent war – a reference to the Ivancich estate – leading Cantwell to reflect that it was a mistake for Venetians to have had any church or villa frescoed by Giotto, Piero della Francesca or Mantegna anywhere near a bridge which might be a strategic target. "Do you know a lot about painters sir?" the driver asks, to which Cantwell replies, "quite a little", adding that he has seen the house where Titian was supposedly born ("not much of a place"). Jackson's only views on Italian art are that there are too many pictures of the Madonna and child, though the painters "were probably big bambini lovers like all Italians".

They pass through the "cheerful town" of San Dona di Piave, a contrast with the "miserable and gloomy" Fossalta just up the river. This leads the colonel to recall that he had recently – like Hemingway – "gone out along the sunken road to find the place where he had been hit, out on the riverbank", at a point where the river was slow and "muddy blue", with reeds along the edges. The crater on the bend of the river, heavy with autumn rain, had been cropped by sheep or goats, "until it looked like a designed depression in a golf course".

No one being in sight Cantwell had squatted down and "relieved himself" (as Hemingway had wanted to do) at the exact spot where "by triangulation" he reckoned he had been badly wounded thirty years previously. He then dug a hole with his Solingen clasp knife "such as German poachers carry" and buried a brown 10,000-lire note (ten times the sum Hemingway himself claimed he had actually buried), to pay for his war medals, symbolising "fertility, blood, money and iron".

"We fought along here when I was a kid", Cantwell tells Jackson when he returns to the car. As a parting gesture he spits in the river: "It was a long spit and he just made it." This is not, as might be supposed, an act of contempt. Rather it is an act of closure, for as a young man at the front, with Austrian guns just yards away, Cantwell (Hemingway) was unable to spit, the fear drying up his throat. "I couldn't spit that night nor afterwards for a long time", he tells Jackson.

And now he can. The novel, set over a long weekend, is in effect one long flashback which returns to the present at the very end, when Cantwell dies of a heart attack on the way back to Trieste after heavy consumption of champagne and Valpolicella while in Venice on top of his heart disease pills. But the core of the novel is his infatuation with Renata. It is, as Hemingway himself remarked, a story of death – but also of love.

18

Love in a Gondola

"Only tourists and lovers take gondolas"

Across the River and Into the Trees

*A*CROSS THE RIVER AND INTO THE TREES bears comparison with Thomas Mann's *Death in Venice*, but has arguably been misunderstood and underestimated. Initial reviews were negative, with even fans of Hemingway disappointed by what they saw as the novel's self-indulgent slow pace and lack of plot. Cantwell himself is an unlikeable character, much given to self-regard as he reminisces in Harry's Bar about his wartime exploits, with Renata as an unlikely teenage admirer hanging on his every word (though she twice – understandably – falls asleep).

Mary Hemingway – who had reasons of her own for being critical – found Colonel Cantwell's conversations with Renata "banal beyond reason", but hoped an editor at Scribner's (his publisher) would improve matters (she was not mollified when Hemingway dedicated the novel to her, "with love".) Cantwell's conceit that he is head of a mythical masonic-style organisation called the Order of Brusadelli, with the head waiter at the Gritti (who plays along with the fantasy) as its *Gran Maestro*, becomes something of a tired joke.

But Hemingway is using here once again the "iceberg theory" of writing fiction, in which the real story takes place just below the surface. We are never told, for example, why Cantwell has been demoted to the rank of colonel from general. As David Hughes has observed, Hemingway "left so much unsaid in his stories that they say far more than you think".

Hemingway himself explained what he had tried to do by saying the book started slowly, but then built up layers of emotion to the point where "you can't stand it, then we level off, so we won't have to provide oxygen tents for the readers". He was baffled when critics complained that "nothing happened" in the novel: "all that happens is the defense of the lower Piave, the breakthrough in Normandy, the taking of Paris and the destruction of the 22nd Inf. Reg. in Hurtgen forest plus a man who loves a girl and dies". That, he felt, was plenty.

Tennessee Williams agreed, writing in *The New York Times* "I could not go to Venice, now, without hearing the haunted cadences of Hemingway's new novel." It was "the saddest novel in the world about the saddest city", and "the best and most honest work that Hemingway has done". Readers would think him crazy for saying so, and critics might treat it "pretty roughly. But its hauntingly tired cadences are the direct speech of a man's heart who is speaking directly for the first time, and that makes it, for me, the finest thing Hemingway has done." As Mark Cirino notes in his astute analysis of the novel, while critics complained that Colonel Cantwell was too much like Hemingway, Renata a "wish fulfillment", the book too "talky" and the prose style "self parodic", admirers responded that, even if this was not the epic they had been expecting, Hemingway's powers of description and ear for dialogue were unchanged, the duck hunt which frames the novel was "beautifully written" and the author's love for Venice was "unmistakable and effectively conveyed".

Sergio Perosa, Professor Emeritus of English and American Literature at Venice University, also finds *Across The River* "a very interesting book" and one preferable to a number of other later Hemingway works. "If I had to choose between *Across the River and Into the Trees* and *For Whom the Bell Tolls*", Perosa told me, "I would choose the former, without a doubt. It is a novel full of sensitivity toward Venice which skilfully uses the city and the lagoon as settings for introspection on love and death". It is deliberately "silent about some things and explicit about others. What Hemingway leaves out is as important as what he puts in."

The novel is above all a tribute to Venice, once "the queen of the seas": "Christ I love it", Cantwell reflects to himself, adding, "I'm so happy I helped defend it when I was a punk kid". Cantwell even gives Jackson a history lesson as they admire the former Cathedral of Santa Maria Assunta on the island of Torcello, explaining that it was "the Torcello boys" who after being driven out of "a little place up the coast called Caorle" by the Visigoths, Lombards and other "bandits" had later decided to build Venice on stilts because the lagoons and the mouth of the Sile River were silting up, breeding mosquitoes and malaria.

Cantwell also explains that the remains of St Mark were located in Alexandria by a "Torcello boy" and smuggled to Venice and its Byzantine cathedral (which Jackson, who knows St Mark's square is where the pigeons are, describes as being like a "moving picture palace"). Like a tourist guide, Cantwell also points out the "lovely campanile" or belltower on Burano, a "very over-populated island" where the women make wonderful lace, and Murano, where the men make wonderful glass "for the rich of all the world" during the day and at night either "make bambinis" or go duck hunting on the lagoon. "Now when you look past Murano you see Venice. That's my town."

He even dreams of retiring there: "I could read in the mornings and walk around town before lunch and go every day to see the Tintorettos at the Accademia and go to the Scuola San Rocco and eat in good cheap joints behind the market, or maybe the woman that ran the house would cook in the evenings." On the Grand Canal he identifies the palazzo where Lord Byron lodged and "slept with the gondolier's wife" two floors below. Byron was nonetheless well loved, being "a tough boy", Cantwell suggests, whereas Robert Browning and his wife Elizabeth Barrett Browning, who also lived on the Grand Canal, were not, because they were "not Venetians no matter how well he wrote of it".

Later in the novel he visits the fish market near the Rialto, which Hemingway himself loved. On the slippery stone floor, in baskets and rope-handled boxes he sees soles, "heavy, grey-green lobsters" destined to die in boiling water, prawns, eels and clams, which he buys "for a pittance" and opens with a curved knife, "cutting close against the shell" and drinking the juice.

His own home, inevitably, is the Gritti Palace, a "three storey, rose-coloured, small, pleasant palace abutting on the Canal. It had been a dependence of the Grand Hotel but now it was its own hotel and a very good one. It was probably the best hotel if you did not wish to be fawned on, or fussed over, or over-flunkied in a city of great hotels, and the Colonel loved it."

He also loves the nearby church of Santa Maria del Giglio, which looks as if it will become airborne at any moment; the beautiful girls "with their long, easy striding Venetian legs"; and the shops, "the charcuterie with the Parmesan cheeses and the hams from San Daniele and the sausages *alla cacciatora* and the bottles of good Scotch whisky and real Gordon's gin". When Hemingway started the story, Mary says, she told him, "Please don't let it be just ducks and marshes. Please put in Venice too." He did – and the Venice he described next to the Gritti Palace is still there.

He would probably be taken aback by the tens of thousands of tourists who nowadays crowd into the lagoon city, the loss of many of the food shops he described and their replacement by tourist gift shops, and the entry charge of 3 Euros for the Giglio Church. But the jewellery shop which Renata and the Colonel visit in the novel, and where in real life Hemingway bought Mary a necklace, is still there, and the magic he felt can still be encountered when you cross a bridge and unexpectedly find yourself in a hidden *campo* (*piazza*) or by the side of a small canal with a magnificent if crumbling palazzo.

But if *Across the River and Into the Trees* is a declaration of love for Venice, it is also a love letter to a woman. It was Hemingway's first novel since *For Whom the Bell Tolls* ten years earlier, and clearly owes its very existence to Adriana, who even designed the dust jacket. She acknowledged that she was the model for Renata. But she always denied that she and Hemingway had made love – rather as Agnes had denied having sex with Hemingway all those years ago in Milan.

The Contessa Renata of the novel (we never learn her surname) is more than a character, she is a symbol of impossible love – and perhaps an agent of death, with the gondola as a floating hearse. "How would you like to be a girl of nineteen years old in love with a man over fifty years old that you know was going to die?" she asks Cantwell at one point. When they meet at Harry's Bar and drink a succession of ice-cold Martinis with garlic olives, it becomes clear they already know each other – though we are not told when or how – and that an affair is already under way, though with more passion on his part than hers.

When Cantwell tells her she is beautiful and he loves her, Renata replies, "You always say that and I don't know what it means but I like to hear it." At the Gritti they kiss by the open window in his room: "The Colonel ... felt her wonderful, long, lithe and properly built body against his own body." She asks him to kiss her again, "and make the buttons of your uniform hurt me but not too much". They do not make love, Renata telling the colonel she has "a disappointment", presumably meaning that she is menstruating.

Renata tells Cantwell she loves him, and promises to marry him and give him five sons. At the hotel they dine on Dalmatian lobster and steak accompanied by Capri Bianco, Valpolicella and Roederer champagne. Cantwell calls Renata "Daughter", and appears to be the dominant figure, given their age difference. But when they take the gondola ride at night, with a bottle of wine in an ice bucket, it is Renata who chooses the gondolier and the route, and sits like "the figure head of a ship", her hair blowing in the wind.

Then under the army blanket on the gondola Cantwell runs his "hurt hand" over her "upraised breasts" – though the flowery elliptical language ("his ruined hand searched for the island in the great river with the high steep banks" ... "the great bird had flown far out of the closed window of the gondola") appears to mean that they stop short of making love, the rather strained metaphors (to quote Mark Cirino) implying that the colonel brings Renata to orgasm manually. She offers to spend the night with him at the Gritti Palace, but he tells her it "wouldn't be right" either for her or for the hotel: instead he has a portrait of her brought to his room and talks to it.

The day after the gondola ride Cantwell and Renata meet for breakfast at Florian's, but the colonel finds St Mark's square flooded and "sad". They return to the Gritti, where Cantwell assures Renata that his last wife has been exorcised from his memory following their divorce – she was a journalist who had only married him to have better contacts, ambitious but talentless, he tells her (presumably an unkind dig at Pauline), using the line from Marlowe which haunted Hemingway all his life: "But that was in another country, and besides the wench is dead."

After they say goodbye, with Renata in tears, Cantwell takes her portrait with him on the road back to Trieste. But his final instruction to his driver Jackson, when he realises he is about to die, is to return the painting and the shotguns he has borrowed from Baron Alvarito for duck shooting back to the Gritti Palace hotel, "where they will be claimed by their rightful owner".

"Adriana was one of the most beautiful women in Italy, and Hemingway fell in love with her", Gianfranco Ivancich once said. "That's it. He called her 'daughter', though it was more like the relationship between a grandfather and granddaughter." "For my sister it was a platonic friendship and nothing more", Adriana and Gianfranco's brother Giacomo told *Il Giornale* in 2014, his memory of Hemingway's intimate involvement with his family still vivid at the age of 82.

For Giacomo, who had a long and distinguished career as an Italian diplomat, the "notorious" love scene in the gondola was a scandal which his family had to endure for years. But it was "pure literary fantasy", he insisted. Adriana's relationship with Hemingway was romantic but above all "spiritual" and idealised. Gianfranco Ivancich also repeated many times that his sister's relationship with Hemingway had been platonic.

But then Renata is also a symbol of Venice, which is itself a symbol of feminine allure. Renata says she has "risen from the sea". But *Across the River* is, in the end, a meditation on how to face death, with Venice as a labyrinthine Isle of the Dead. As John Paul Russo has pointed out, the novel begins and ends in the swamp on which Venice is built, a traditional Western symbol for "pollution, disease and death". Cantwell looks back at what he has lost – his women, his youth, his health, his generalship – and defies death while at the same time longing for it, conceiving death as a process of watery decomposition.

"Yesterday I died with my Colonel for the last time and said goodbye to the girl", Hemingway wrote to Marlene Dietrich from the Hotel Gritti on 1 July 1950 after putting the final touches to the novel. The Colonel has – like Hemingway himself – revisited the place where he was wounded in the First World War. But if this is an attempt to ward off decay and decomposition it does not work in the novel, any more than it did in real life.

At the start of the novel, as Cantwell and Jackson are entering

Venice, they pass the boats and fishing nets on the canal carrying water from the Brenta, and he thinks of the "long stretch of the Brenta where the great villas were, with their lawns and their gardens and the plane trees and the cypresses. I'd like to be buried out there, he thought. I know the place very well."

19

The White Tower

"I simply uncorked the bottle"

Adriana Ivancich

IN APRIL 1949 the Hemingways returned to Cuba on the *Jagiello* from Genoa, where Fernanda Pivano found Mary packing an "enormous bag" with Venetian glass and lace as souvenirs of their trip.

In Havana they were visited by Nanuk Franchetti, and by Adriana's brother Gianfranco, who in return for help with his visa (and Martinis "made almost purely of gin") corrected errors in Italian language and geography in the typescript of *Across the River and Into the Trees*. In the end Gianfranco became something of a permanent fixture at the Finca, staying there for three years before buying a farm with Hemingway's help (the loan was repaid) and meeting a Cuban girl, Marquise Cristina Sandoval y de la Torriente, a descendant of the Spanish Conquistadores whom he married in 1956.

On this occasion the Havana interlude did not last long however. In November 1949 Hemingway travelled to New York to make the sea journey across the Atlantic back to Europe, though not before holding a supper party where the guests included Marlene Dietrich in a full-length mink coat. He sailed back to Le Havre with Mary on the *Ile de France* on 19 November and they headed for Paris and the Ritz, where he worked on *Across the River*. They then returned to Venice – this time in a Packard with a new driver, Georges – via Paris, Avignon, Nice and Nervi on the Italian Riviera, where they spent New Year's Eve.

They again met up with the Franchettis and the Kechlers, and entertained their friends – including Adriana – at the Locanda Cipriani on Torcello. Hemingway, Arrigo Cipriani later recalled, would often write all night at the Locanda and then sleep late. Cipriani's aunt Gabriella, who ran the restaurant, told the waiters to keep their voices down so as not to wake Hemingway, especially if there were more than three empty bottles of Amarone di Valpolicella outside his room. His favourite food at lunch or dinner was risotto and fried fish followed by crepes.

Mary was tolerant of Hemingway's platonic infatuation with Adriana, at whom he often gazed during the long meals with friends as if lovestruck. But she was rather more wary of "predatory females" such as Princess Aspasia, mother of King Peter of Yugoslavia, who offered to build Hemingway a "special house" in her garden if he would live there.

In February 1950 Hemingway and Mary went back to Cortina, and stayed two weeks, this time at the Hotel Posta. Mary went skiing while Hemingway stayed in bed writing. In a spate of bad luck Ernest developed another skin infection, for which he was given penicillin, and Mary again broke her ankle (this time the left one) while skiing and spent three weeks in a cast.

The Hemingways returned to Paris and then the US and Cuba from Le Havre on the *Ile de France* on 21 March 1950 – seen off, somewhat to Mary's irritation, by Adriana, who made the long journey to Le Havre with a girlfriend. Back in Havana Hemingway published two childrens' stories for *Holiday* magazine, illustrated by Adriana: 'The Good Lion', written for Adriana's nephew Gherardo Scapinelli (the son of her sister Francesca), which features an African lion who eats pasta and scampi and has wings which enable him to fly to Venice, and 'The Faithful Bull', written for the daughter of Carlo di Robilant.

Whilst helping Gianfranco get a job with a shipping company, Hemingway wrote to Adriana in June 1950, adding "Am prejudiced about you because I am in love with you ... I love you very much." "I will always love you in my heart and I cannot help that", he wrote the same month in a letter signed "Mister Papa", which Adriana reproduced in her memoir. But he would try not to say it to her personally or even write it again in a letter. "All I will try to do is try to serve you well and be happy company when we meet ... I get terribly lonely for you sometimes so it is unbearable. But if there is nothing to be done about that there is nothing to be done." Gianfranco, he told Buck Lanham, was "the brother of a girl I know in Venice (a town I left my heart in and haven't been able to find the son of a bitch yet)".

But Hemingway was suffering from moods of depression and melancholy, aggravated by his irritation over negative reviews of *Across the River*, even though the *TLS* compared its "swan song mood" to Sophocles and Shakespeare and it was praised by old army buddies, including Buck Lanham. Always accident prone, he slipped on his boat, the Pilar, while on a fishing trip and suffered a deep scalp wound as well as pains in his swollen right leg: an x-ray found fragments of the 1918 mortar shell.

Adriana, who had designed the front cover for the US edition of *Across the River*, a drawing of a Venetian canal, arrived in Havana in October 1950 on the *Luciano Manara*, chaperoned as ever by her mother Dora. "If Ernest's eyes misted over with emotion, I did not see it", Mary wrote in her memoirs. She had been less than keen on the visit – "the idea of two Venetian ladies traipsing down to Cuba to visit us seemed utterly irrational to me" – and when Hemingway suggested it she insisted that the invitation come from both of them, "for propriety".

For Adriana the sight of the Cuban coastline that late October morning – "the new world" – was a moment of "great emotion". Her happiness was tinged with sadness, however: "if it had not been for Gianfranco, Papa Hemingway and Mary, I would have been happy to sail on like that for years, perhaps – who knows – forever".

Hemingway was careful never to be alone with Adriana. Instead she stayed in the guesthouse, a tower, with her pencils and paints, and Hemingway told her they were equal partners in 'White Tower Inc'. Her presence inspired him to take up *The Old Man and the Sea* – said to be based on Gregorio Fuentes, the first mate of his fishing boat, the Pilar – after sixteen years and complete it.

It was now that Hemingway's son Gregory found her lovely, according to his later account of his father, *Papa*. She was rather dull, he thought (Hemingway did not tell her that bit), but undoubtedly attractive with dark hair, dark eyes, high cheekbones, a "thin but not too angular face" and "a lovely smile that betrayed no conceit or over-awareness of her lineage". Hemingway kept stroking her hand, gave a dinner dance in her honour, but went no further.

Cubans found this rather pathetic. Mario Menocal, a friend in Havana, said Adriana was "very good-looking, super-sexy in a very Italian way" as well as bright and witty, and was able to "run rings" round her older admirer. The result, Menocal thought, according to Jeffrey Meyers, was that Hemingway was made to look a fool with his "fawning, self-deceiving attitude": she accepted his hospitality and generosity but "gave nothing in return".

Mary meanwhile continued to put up with Hemingway's infatuation, turning the other cheek even when in a fit of temper (made worse by the poor reviews for *Across the River*) he hurled Mary's typewriter on the floor and threw wine in her face while Adriana and her mother were at the Finca.

For Dora the last straw was a letter she received from a friend in Venice telling her that the talk of the town was Hemingway's portrayal of Adriana as Renata in *Across the River and Into the Trees*, and in particular the love scene with the Colonel in the gondola. "We must leave here immediately", Dora told her daughter. In vain Adriana protested that she had never been in a gondola with Hemingway: "You are still only a girl and I have to defend your reputation" was her mother's firm reply.

The two Ivancich women moved to a hotel, and returned to Italy in February 1951 after a stay in Cuba of some four months. "What happened when we met is a little more than a romance", Adriana wrote later. "I broke down his defenses: he stopped drinking when I asked him to. I am proud to say that I led him to write *The Old Man and The Sea* ... He said words flowed out of him easily thanks to me. I simply uncorked the bottle."

It was a pity, Mary said as Adriana and Dora left Cuba, that Hemingway had not taken her advice and portrayed Renata as a red-haired girl from Trieste so as to avoid any possible identification with Adriana. Yes, Adriana concluded, but "a novel is a novel", and if people insist on finding real-life parallels "where the devil does that leave the freedom of the writer?"

"A novel is a novel". Yet the relationship with Adriana nonetheless caused scandalised gossip, which Adriana bore in silence. It was only many years later, in 1980, that she gave her side of the story in her Italian-language memoir entitled – appropriately enough – *La Torre Bianca*, or *The White Tower*. "Naturally he wrote it for me, thinking of me", she said of *Across the River*, "but I didn't like the book and told him so".

After an unsuccessful first marriage, Adriana married a German count named Rudolf von Rex and had two sons by him. They lived on a farm near Orbetello on the Tuscan coast, where in the distant 1920s Hemingway and his then wife Hadley had joined Ezra and Dorothy Pound on the trail of the Italian *condottiere* Sigismondo Malatesta. Maintaining a palazzo in Venice, Adriana said, was out of the question: "It is the general Venetian tragedy – pollution, foundations crumbling, walls falling to pieces."

She continued to maintain that she and Hemingway had only ever kissed: "He never did the slightest thing that might oblige me to be defensive", she said, a denial uncannily reminiscent of Agnes von Kurowsky's protests that she had not had sex with Hemingway back in 1918 ("I was not that kind of girl"). The love scene under the blanket in the gondola was pure invention, Adriana said. In *La Torre Bianca* Adriana admits she told a handsome young friend of her brother's to whom she was attracted that although she was not Renata, the physical description of the character was based on her. But she had never considered marriage to Hemingway, who had once asked her to be his wife but was married already, and who was in any case "too old. It was unthinkable." Hemingway however continued to write her effusive letters, writing at one point, "I love you more than the moon and the sky and for as long as I shall live."

Mary took it all philosophically, describing the idea that her husband had proposed to Adriana as "nonsense". "Ernest was fond of her, as he was fond of quite a few young women. He certainly didn't make this one a problem for me." Although Venetian parents were strict, she wrote in her article about Harry's Bar and its clientele, they allowed their daughters to go to the bar because "all Venice would know at once if they misbehaved". In 1949, she recalled, Hemingway had flirted at Harry's Bar with "a striking beauty" sipping orange juice. He was accosted by yet another of his aristocratic friends, Prince Tassilo Furstenberg, who remarked "I see you've made friends with my daughter Ira." It turned out later that Ira was 14.

Another of Hemingway's teenage Venetian friends was Afdera Franchetti, the sister of Nanuk. Afdera claimed that she, together with Adriana, was the model for Renata, and that the character was a composite portrait of both of them. Hemingway, she said, was in love with her, she had visited him in Cuba, and they had spent a month together in Paris, winning millions of francs at the Auteuil racecourse. Hemingway found all this amusing, telling Adriana that Afdera (who later married the actor Henry Fonda) had to be allowed her fantasies.

To spare Adriana embarrassment, Hemingway had forbidden the publication of *Across the River and Into the Trees* in Italian for at least two years: in the event it was not issued in Italy until 1965. He never saw Adriana again after their last meeting in June 1954 at the Hotel Savoia Beeler in Nervi on the Italian Riviera, where Hemingway and Mary spent the night before boarding a ship back to Havana. She published a volume of poetry, but her second marriage was no happier than her first. In 1983 she took her own life and is buried at Porto Ercole, in Tuscany.

Thirty years earlier, in 1953, her volume of poetry was published by Mondadori – Hemingway's own Italian publisher – entitled *I Have Seen Heaven and Earth* (*Ho guardato il cielo e la terra*). The setting of much of the verse is inevitably Venice, with sympathetic and perceptive portrayals of fishermen, soldiers and gypsies. But there are also intensely personal reflections: of the murder of her father, Carlo, she writes, "*Per la prima volta/avevamo dovuto comprendere/il valore del tempo/e che le favole non esistono piu*" – "For the first time we were made to understand the value of time/and that fairy tales no longer exist."

Despite her natural reserve Adriana's verses, the Venetian literary critic Gian Antonio Cibotto wrote, reveal her sensations and states of mind with "open self-disclosure". "*Ti ringrazio, mio caro amico*" runs one verse, "*perche quando mi guardi negli occhi tu credi in me*" – "I thank you, my dear friend, because when you look into my eyes, you believe in me."

20

Scampi and Valpolicella

"Since trip to Italy have been studying the life of Dante. Seems to be one of the worst jerks that ever lived, but how well he could write! This may be a lesson to us all"

Hemingway to John Dos Passos, 17 September 1949

ITALY WAS STILL ON HEMINGWAY's mind in the 1950s. "We have lovely weather now and the sky is almost like Italy", he wrote in October 1952 to Bernard Berenson, who had praised *The Old Man and the Sea* as "a short but not small masterpiece". "I ought to be in Italy now", Hemingway added, "but I have to try to run my life so that it does not ruin everyone else's life. But this is when I miss Italy the most."

In 1953 he set off first for Spain, despite his fear that he might be detained because of the Republican sympathies he had displayed. Gianfranco and the Kechlers' driver, Adamo De Simon, met the Hemingways at Le Havre on 30 June 1953 in a Lancia Aurelia, and after loading a "mountain of bags" on top of it they drove to Madrid by way of Chartres, Poitiers and the Loire Valley.

In Madrid he stayed at the Hotel Florida – which had been the journalists' bolt hole during the Spanish Civil War, and the scene of his affair with Martha Gellhorn – and admired the paintings at the Prado, especially Andrea del Sarto's *Portrait of a Woman*, which reminded him of Adriana. In the Sierra de Guadarrama he showed Mary the bridge Robert Jordan and his fellow anti-Franco guerrillas blow up in *For Whom the Bell Tolls*, persuading himself that he had actually fought in the civil war instead of simply reporting it.

He then returned to France, taking a ship in August 1953 from Marseilles via Genoa to Mombasa in Kenya. Hemingway's son Patrick had used his inheritance from Pauline to buy a farm in East Africa, running safaris with the help of Philip Percival, a noted big game hunter (the 'Pop' of *Green Hills of Africa*). The safari went well, at least for Hemingway: he shot rhinos, lions and zebras, hunted leopards with a spear and enjoyed wild nights with a Masai girl called Debba while Mary was in Nairobi. He and Mary then flew in a Cessna to Mwanza on Lake Victoria and then to Bukavu in the Congo, and headed for the Murchison Falls on the Nile in Uganda.

But the Cessna crashed three miles from the Falls when their pilot swerved to avoid a flock of ibis and struck an old telegraph wire. The pilot warned them they were going to crash: "I turned my face away from the windshield and covered my eyes with my arms", Mary wrote later in her memoirs. "In rending, smashing, crashing noises we came to a stop among low trees and bushes." Hemingway had hurt his right shoulder, and both were in shock.

They spent the night in the bush above the river listening to the elephants and drinking Scotch and beer. The next morning they were rescued by a launch which happened to be passing and took them to Lake Albert. A bush pilot offered them a replacement plane at Butiaba, a De Havilland Rapide, but it caught fire on take off and crashed. Mary escaped through a window, hurting her knee and cracking two ribs, while Ernest forced his way through a jammed door, using his head as a battering ram and badly injuring his skull, shoulders, spine, liver and kidneys.

After reaching Lake Victoria and then Nairobi the Hemingways sailed from Mombasa to Port Said, with Hemingway reading with interest the obituaries of him which newspapers had published in the belief that he was dead, several of which suggested he had "sought death all his life". In fact he very nearly had died: he had sustained serious injuries to his head, kidneys, intestines and spine, with a ruptured liver, temporary loss of vision and hearing, and first-degree burns on his face and arms.

Before leaving Africa he – amazingly – dictated an article for *Look* magazine (which had sponsored the trip), went fishing and tried to help firefighters dealing with a bush fire only to stumble and sustain further burns on his body. It was time to leave Africa – and the only possible destination was Venice and the Gritti Palace.

At Venice in April 1954 Hemingway underwent extensive examination of his damaged vertebrae and kidneys. The worst part was having a ruptured kidney ("much blood and pieces of kidney in urine", he wrote to Bernard Berenson). He boasted to Adriana – by now 24 – that unlike Henry James, who in Venice had merely looked out of a window and smoked a cigar, he was still active despite being ill, making trips to Torcello and Codroipo (which he did).

In reality, however, he spent most of his time in his room at the Gritti Palace in pyjamas, an old sweater and carpet slippers, wearing an eyeshade. It was now that he invented the ideal Venetian 'cure' while recuperating – scampi and Valpolicella – although the hotel acknowledges that this was "not so much a medical cure as good for the soul". The 'Hemingway menu' nowadays offered by the hotel is rather fuller, consisting of scampi risotto and shellfish consomme followed by duck cooked with ginger and honey in a port sauce, a chocolate dessert with Bourbon and *friandises* or *petits fours* of preserved fruits, sweets and biscuits, all accompanied by Soave as well as Valpolicella. Hemingway wrote in the Gritti Palace guest book: "To our home in Venice".

Valpolicella, made in the Monti Lissini foothills near Verona and Lake Garda, is noted for its light-bodied fragrance. Wine, Hemingway wrote in *Death in the Afternoon*, was "one of the most civilized things in the world and one of the natural things of the world that has been brought to the greatest perfection, and it offers a greater range of enjoyment and appreciation than, possibly, any other purely sensory thing which may be purchased". He loved "the honesty and delicacy" of wine, and "the light body of it on your tongue, cool in your mouth and warm when you have drunk it". He was especially fond of Amarone, a ripe and full-bodied variety of Valpolicella.

Even Valpolicella failed to do the trick after the African disaster however. His friend Aaron Hotchner was shocked when he saw Hemingway. Any hair which had not been burned had turned white, as had his beard, and "he appeared to have diminished somewhat – I don't mean physically diminished, but some of the aura of massiveness seemed to have gone out him".

His tendency to confuse fact and fiction became worse. He gave Hotchner and other friends in Venice a graphic description of having been to bed with the glamorous exotic dancer and double agent Mata Hari, even though she was arrested and executed in 1917, the year before he arrived in Italy at the age of 18. It was shortly after this that he told Hotchner that his First World War affair with a Red Cross nurse had been in Turin rather than Milan, which may or may not have been a similar flight of fancy.

But he was still able to enjoy a trip in April 1954 in the Lancia Aurelia with Federico Kechler and the Kechler driver Adamo De Simon to Udine, where he was feted by a gathering of local writers and artists at the Hotel Friuli. On 15 April the party headed for Latisana and one of Hemingway's favourite restaurants, *La Bella Venezia* (still there, though in a different location) before driving (or being driven) fifteen kilometres south to Lignano, a sandy beach at the mouth of the Tagliamento which Alberto Kechler was developing as a resort together with a consortium of like-minded entrepreneurs.

The Kechlers had once ridden horses along the beach at Lignano, and could see its potential as post-war tourism began to develop. Lignano – now in effect three resorts: Lignano Pineta, Lignano Riviera and Lignano Sabbiadoro (meaning Golden Sand) – was designed by the celebrated Friuli architect and urban planner Marcello D'Olivo as a series of concentric circles hidden among the seaside pines, rather than the conventional grid system of streets. It was, Hemingway declared, the "Italian Florida". He only stayed in Lignano for two hours, but it was enough for the resort to later inaugurate a ten-acre "Hemingway Park" planted with pine trees, orchids and roses, with a bust of the writer, unveiled in 1984 by his glamorous granddaughter, the actress Margaux Hemingway.

It also offers a literary Hemingway Prize, awarded every year. Lignano is even twinned with Ketchum, Hemingway's last home in Idaho, and offers trips by boat up the Tagliamento River to Latisana, the scene of his first encounter with Adriana Ivancich. Lignano, says Giorgio Ardito, who heads the resort's management company, Lignano Pineta Spa, is thriving, with a winter population of 6000 which swells to 150,000 in summer.

"Hemingway thought of buying a seaside house here", he says. "He even put his signature on a plot of land on the development plan." A charming photograph of the time shows Hemingway (in suit and tie) and Federico Kechler's wife Maria Luisa on the beach shaking sand from their shoes. But he never came back.

21

Death in Ketchum

"Tutti mi chiamano bionda"

Popular gondoliers' song

THE FOLLOWING MONTH, May 1954, Hemingway left Venice for Milan, after a farewell party held for him at the Ivancichs' palazzo in Venice. The route was no longer the romantic landscape he had hoped for however, with its "vulgar and awful" billboards. At the Hotel Principe in Milan he called on Ingrid Bergman, who was performing as Joan of Arc at La Scala, but took a dislike to her lover, Roberto Rossellini, who he called "a 22-pound rat".

He then travelled to Turin and Cuneo with Hotchner, and down to Nice. Buying a bottle of Scotch at Cuneo, he was nearly crushed by admirers when recognised, and had to be rescued by a squad of soldiers. In Nice he wrote a letter to Adriana at five in the morning, as the sun was coming up: "Daughter you know how I miss you and leaving was like an amputation. Thank you for being so good and lovely to me."

From Nice he went to Spain, praying at Burgos cathedral on his knees despite his injuries, and then returned to Italy, to Genoa, to take the ship back to Havana. But first Hemingway and Mary went along the Riviera coast to the Italian resort of Alassio, which had an

English colony and in the 1950s was much frequented by the newly emerging "jet set" of *la dolce vita*.

Hemingway had visited Alassio several times before, starting in 1948. It was "the one nice town on the Italian Riviera", he told his friend AE Hotchner. Hemingway and Mary had stayed several times at the Swiss-owned Hotel Savoia Beeler at Nervi, close to Genoa; the hotel is now apartments, but the local history society still preserves Mary's notes thanking the management for its hospitality, dated 25 November 1948, New Year's Day 1950 and 6 June 1954. He was also fond of the bars and restaurants of Santa Margherita Ligure and Portofino.

On his first trip in 1948 Hemingway had run out of whisky and searched the Riviera in vain for his favourite tipple, The Antiquary, a twelve-year-old blended Scotch whisky named after Sir Walter Scott's Gothic novel about buried treasure. He eventually found it at the Caffe Roma, a piano bar near the Alassio seafront run by a local painter named Mario Berrino, who later said, "We had a case of it, I have no idea why."

Hemingway, according to Berrino, drank a bottle of The Anti-quary "in a few hours", and returned to Alassio several times to polish off the rest of the case, often sleeping off the effects on the beach. Berrino kept an autograph book for celebrities to sign, and had the idea of transferring the autographs instead onto coloured ceramic tiles on the wall ("Muretto") of the nearby public gardens. Hemingway at first had doubts, suggesting it would look like "a collection of epitaphs", but added "unless each one was different from the others" and eventually told Berrino (no doubt after a few more drinks) "Mario, you have to do it."

They put the tiles up at dawn, since they had no official approval at the time. Hemingway's signature was one of the first to be displayed, together with tiles commemorating the musicians who provided the soundtrack of the time, the vocal group Quartetto Cetra and the jazz guitarist Cosimo di Ceglie. The tile featuring Hemingway's signature is undated: a portrait of him with his much-loved parrot Pedrito on his arm bears the date 2 July 1951, when he was in Cuba, not Italy, but was presumably placed on the wall when the scheme was sanctioned by the mayor.

The first tiles are still there, together with those of Anita Ekberg, Jean Cocteau, Vittorio De Sica, Dario Fo and over five hundred others. In the summer of 1953, after Hemingway had commented on the attractiveness of the local girls, Berrino followed up his "wall of autographs" by launching a Miss Muretto beauty contest. He also inherited Pedrito, whose fortieth birthday in 1988 was also immortalised in a ceramic tile. Remarkably the parrot survived for nearly half a century, until 1994.

The 1954 trip to Alassio was to be Hemingway's last. "I remember he had his arm in a sling after the aircraft accident in Africa", Berrino told *La Stampa* in 1999. Asked for his abiding memories of Hemingway, Berrino replied that the writer, far from being a braggart, "listened a lot and said little". Neither was he a "miser or stingy": on the contrary he was generous, and had once given a poor fisherman who hung around the bar but could not afford a drink a handful of dollars, much to the puzzlement of the fisherman, who had never seen US money before.

Hemingway was 55, and about to be awarded the Nobel Prize for Literature, which he accepted "with humility". The citation praised his "manly love of danger and adventure", his admiration for any individual who "fights the good fight in a world of reality overshadowed by violence and death", and above all his pioneering "mastery of the art of modern narration". Writing, he responded from Havana, was a "lonely life"; each book was a "new beginning", with the writer having to "face eternity, or the lack of it, each day".

Hemingway's final stories in the fifties include 'Get Yourself a Seeing Eyed Dog', the sentimental tale of an American going blind in Venice, probably inspired by his own erysipelas in 1949. He returned several times to Paris and to Spain, but growing ill health – coupled with heavy drinking – ruled out a final trip to Africa. Back in Havana, he wrote sketches of his time in Paris in the 1920s with Gertrude Stein, Ezra Pound and Scott Fitzgerald, based on several trunks of his youthful notes and other papers which had been found stored at the Ritz. This would become *A Moveable Feast*.

But Cuba was becoming politically unstable and heading for civil war – "both sides atrocious", Hemingway wrote – and he longed for the wide open spaces of the American Midwest. He moved with Mary to the mining town of Ketchum in the hunting and fishing resort of Sun Valley, Idaho, which he had first come to know with Martha Gellhorn.

He divided his time between Ketchum and Havana, where he at first welcomed the Castro revolution, even kissing the Cuban flag and handing Fidel Castro the prize when El Comandante won a fishing competition in 1960. The Finca, however, was expropriated by the new regime, and eventually became a state museum to Hemingway, though Mary was allowed to remove many of their possessions, including his archive and valuable paintings.

He indulged in one final fling – which, as with Adriana, was almost certainly platonic – with a young girl, this time 19-year-old Valerie Danby-Smith, an Irish would-be reporter he first met in Madrid when she was an inexperienced stringer for a news agency and was sent to interview him. He coached her in journalism and made her his secretary, her obvious devotion to him leading to gossip that they were lovers. Relations between Hemingway and Mary were often strained, and their quarrels were fuelled by drink. Valerie certainly offered Hemingway devotion in his decline, and after his death married his son Gregory, having four children by him.

Hemingway may also have made one final trip to Venice, this time without the watchful Mary's knowledge. In August 1960 he went to

Spain on his own for just over two months, while Mary remained in New York. At the end of May, he had written to Gianfranco Ivancich from Havana about what to do with the Lancia and "the funds" he had left in Venice. He was suffering from growing mental illness and depression; did he perhaps secretly head for the lagoon city of love and death one last time? Intriguingly Baron Alberto Franchetti, who would have been 13 at the time, told me he clearly remembered as a young adolescent running into the shambling figure of Hemingway, the worse for wear, in Calle Vallaresso, near Harry's Bar. Gianfranco's daughter Irina doubts that Hemingway made a final trip to Venice: "After all my father would have known about it, and so would my aunt Adriana. Neither of them ever mentioned it." But then Adriana did not include everything in her memoirs – for example she omitted her meeting with Hemingway at Nervi before he sailed back to Cuba in June 1954, giving the impression that their final encounter was in Venice itself when in fact Hemingway wrote to her from the ship to say she had given him a wonderful surprise by seeing him off. So quite possibly he did make that final trip, perhaps to collect his Italian bank funds and royalties, or even to contemplate ending it all in one of Venice's many canals, drawn – as many suicides have been, and still are – to the city's dream-like beauty combined with an atmosphere of decay, the backdrop to Thomas Mann's *Death in Venice*.

But at the end Hemingway became a recluse at Ketchum, staring across the river through the cottonwoods to the local cemetery. He was by now, according to Gregory, a "paranoid schizophrenic": his conviction that the FBI was spying on him, or at least keeping an eye on him, had some basis in fact, but it now became an obsession. His drinking, always heavy, had become that of a severe alcoholic.

At one point Mary found him standing by the gun rack with a shotgun and two shells: he was persuaded to put them back, and was flown to the Mayo Clinic in Rochester for electro-shock treatment, which only made matters worse. When he returned to the clinic a second time he had to be restrained from committing suicide by walking into a plane's propellers during a stopover in South Dakota.

There had been (and was to be again) a history of suicide in the Hemingway family; he never forgot that his own father had shot himself in 1928. "He was going through that time of a man's life when things are liable to seem the very blackest and most out of proportion too", he wrote at the time to Pauline's mother. Perhaps that was how he himself now felt. When Hemingway returned to Ketchum he was determined to end it: Mary had locked the guns in the basement, but he knew where the keys were, on a ledge above the kitchen sink.

He chose the shotgun he had often used to shoot pigeons, placed the twin barrels against his head, and pulled the trigger. Mary, when the news got out, claimed it had been an accident. It was not, as she admitted five years later to the Italian journalist Oriana Fallaci. The man who had defied death at the Austrian front in Italy in 1918, and many times since then, from Spain to Africa, had killed himself.

The night before Hemingway shot himself he and Mary – according to her diary – began singing a gondoliers' song as they were preparing to go to bed. It was a song they had been taught by Hemingway's Italian translator Fernanda Pivano at Cortina d'Ampezzo: "*Tutti mi chiamano bionda, ma bionda io non sono*" – "Everyone calls me a blonde, but blonde I am not." Hemingway sang the last line – "*Porto i capelli neri*" – "I have black hair."

And so Italy stayed with him to the end. If the Italian landscape, from the Venetian lagoons and marshes to the Dolomites as well as Liguria and Sicily, had a profound effect on him, so too did the Italian people – not just the aristocrats he came to know so well in Venetian high society, but also the ordinary Italians he came across, from soldiers, drivers and waiters to lace makers and hunters. He was a larger-than-life character, and Italy was his equal, stimulating his imagination not only with its elegance, history and beauty but also with its resilience and its love of life. His Italian writings, Hemingway concluded, had "that special something you only get in a love letter". It was a love affair which has left us with enduring masterpieces of literature.

Bibliography

Ackerman, Rich, Colletto, Roberto, Davanzo Dino, Fasan, Marco, and Marcuzzo, Bruno (eds): *Through Harvey's Eyes*. Edizioni Saisera, Udine 2009.

Baker, Carlos: *Ernest Hemingway: A Life Story*. Charles Scribner's Sons, New York 1969.

Baker, Carlos (ed): *Ernest Hemingway, Selected Letters 1917–1961*. Scribner, New York 1981.

Baker, Carlos: *Hemingway, The Writer as Artist*. Princeton University Press 1952.

Beaumont, John: The *Mississippi Flows into the Tiber: A Guide to Notable American Converts to the Catholic Church*. Fidelity Press 2014.

Benson, Jackson J (ed): *New Critical Approaches to the Short Stories of Ernest Hemingway*. Duke University Press 1990.

Burgess, Anthony: *Ernest Hemingway*. Thames and Hudson, London 1978.

Burwell, Rose Marie: *Hemingway: The Post-war Years and The Posthumous Novels*. Cambridge University Press 1996.

Cecchin, Giovanni: *Con Hemingway e Dos Passos sui campi di battaglia italiani della grande guerra*. Mursia, Milan 1980.

Cecchin, Giovanni: *Isonzo, Caporetto e la ritirata. Bassano del Grappa*. Collezione Princeton, Bassano del Grappa 1996.

Cecchin, Giovanni: *Inglesi sull' Altopiano*. Collezione Princeton, Bassano del Grappa 1995.

Cecchin, Giovanni: *Hemingway, Trevelyan e Il Friuli, alle origini di 'Addio alle Armi'*. Lignano Sabbiadoro 1986.

Cecchin, Giovanni: *Hemingway, Americani e Volontariato in Italia nella Grande Guerra*. Collezione Princeton, Bassano del Grappa 1999.

Cirino, Mark: *Ernest Hemingway: Thought in Action*. University of Wisconsin 2012.

Cirino, Mark: *Reading Hemingway's Across the River and Into the Trees*. Kent State University Press 2016.

Cohassey, John: *Hemingway and Pound: A Most Unlikely Friendship*. McFarland and Co, North Carolina 2014.

Cortese, Giandomenico, Fontana, Giovanni Luigi and Pozzato, Paolo (eds): *Hemingway e La Grande Guerra*. Fondazione Luca, Bassano del Grappa 2015.

Curnutt, Kirk: *Coffee with Hemingway*, Foreword by John Updike. Duncan Baird Publishers 2007.

DeFazio, Albert J III (ed): *Dear Papa, Dear Hotch: The Correspondence of Ernest Hemingway and AE Hotchner*. University of Missouri 2005.

Di Scala, Spencer M: *Vittorio Emanuele Orlando*. Haus Publishing, London 2010.

Fenton, Charles A: *The Apprenticeship of Ernest Hemingway*. Farrer, Strauss and Young, New York 1954.

Fussell, Paul: *Uniforms, Why We Are What We Wear*. Houghton Mifflin Co, Boston and New York 2002.

Ghiotto, Edoardo (ed): *Hemingway a Schio*. Menin Edizioni, Schio 2008.

Griffin, Peter: *Along with Youth: Hemingway, The Early Years*. Oxford University Press 1985.

Hall, N John: *Max Beerbohm: A Kind of Life*. Yale University Press 2002.

Hawkins, Ruth: *Unbelievable Happiness and Final Sorrow: The Hemingway-Pfeiffer Marriage*. University of Arkansas Press 2012.

Hemingway, Leicester: *My Brother, Ernest Hemingway*. Pineapple Press 1996.

Hemingway, Mary Welsh: *How It Was*. Weidenfeld and Nicholson, London 1977.

Hemingway, Sean (ed): *Hemingway on War*. Vintage Books, London 2014.

Hemingway, Valerie: *Running With The Bulls: My Years with the Hemingways*. Random House 2006.

Hotchner, AE: *Papa Hemingway: A Personal Memoir*. Da Capo Press 2004.

Hotchner, AE: *Hemingway in Love: His Own Story*. Picador 2015.

Hutchisson, James M: *Hemingway: A New Life*. Penn State University Press 2016.

Ivancich, Gianfranco: *Da una felice Cuba a Ketchum, I miei giorni con Ernest Hemingway*. Edizioni della Laguna 2008.

Kale, Verna: *Ernest Hemingway: A Critical Life*. Reaktion Books 2016.

Knigge, Jobst C: *Hemingway's Venetian Muse Adriana Ivancich A Contribution to the Biography of Ernest Hemingway*. Humboldt University, Berlin 2011.

Knigge, Jobst C: *Hemingway and the Venetian Nobility*. Humboldt University, Berlin 2014.

Leff, Leonard J: *Hemingway and his Conspirators: Hollywood, Scribners and the Making of an American Celebrity Culture*. Rowman and Littlefield 1997.

Lewis, Robert W (ed): *Hemingway in Italy and Other Essays*, Praeger Publishers, New York 1990.

Lorigliola, Davide: *Hemingway e Lignano*. Societa Filologica
   Friuliana, Udine 2014.

Lynn, Kenneth S: *Hemingway*. Harvard University Press 1987.

Mandel, Miriam B: *Reading Hemingway: The Facts in the Fiction*.
   Scarecrow Press 2001.

Messent, Peter: *Ernest Hemingway*. Macmillan, London 1992.

Meyers, Jeffrey: *Hemingway: A Biography*. Macmillan, London
   1986.

Moddelmog, Debra A and del Gizzo, Suzanne (eds): *Ernest
   Hemingway in Context*. Cambridge University Press 2011.

Moorehead, Caroline: *Martha Gellhorn: A Life*. Chatto and
   Windus, London 2003.

Moorehead, Caroline: *Selected Letters of Martha Gellhorn*. Henry
   Holt and Co, New York 2006.

Nickel, Matthew: *Hemingway's Dark Night: Catholic Influences
   and Intertextualities in the Work of Ernest Hemingway*. New
   Street Communications 2013.

Pavan, Camillo: *Sile, alla scoperta del fiume, imaggini, storia,
   itinerari*. Treviso 1989.

Perosa, Sergio (ed): *Hemingway e Venezia*. LS Olschki, Florence
   1988.

Pivano, Fernanda: *Hemingway*. Bompiani 1985.

Pivano, Fernanda: *Tutti I racconti di Ernest Hemingway*.
   Mondadori 2011.

Polo, Matteo: *Da Qui Non Passeranno*. Edizioni del Vento, Jesolo
   Lido 2008.

Reynolds, Michael: *Hemingway: The Paris Years*. WW Norton and
   Co 1989.

Reynolds, Michael: *The Young Hemingway*. WW Norton and Co
   1998.

Reynolds, Michael: *Hemingway: The Homecoming*. WW Norton
   and Co 1992.

Reynolds, Michael: *Hemingway's First War: The Making of 'A Farewell to Arms'*. Princeton University Press 1976.

Riall, Lucy: *Under the Volcano, Revolution in a Sicilian Town*. Oxford University Press 2013.

Sanderson, Rita (ed): *Hemingway's Italy, New Perspectives*. Louisiana State University Press 2006.

Sanderson, Rita, Spanier, Sandra and Trogdon, Robert W (eds): *The Letters of Ernest Hemingway* Volume 1, 1907–1922. Cambridge University Press 2015.

Sanderson, Rita, Spanier, Sandra and Trogdon, Robert W (eds): *The Letters of Ernest Hemingway* Volume 2, 1923–1925. Cambridge University Press 2015.

Sanderson, Rita, Spanier, Sandra and Trogdon, Robert W (eds): *The Letters of Ernest Hemingway* Volume 3, 1926–1929. Cambridge University Press 2015.

Sanford, Marcelline Hemingway: *At the Hemingways: A Family Portrait*. Little, Brown 1962.

Sartor, Ivano: *La Grande Guerra nelle Retrovie*. Dosson di Treviso 1988.

Sartor, Ivano: *Il Centro di Roncade tra Storia e Modernita*. Piazza Editore, Silea 2011.

Sindelar, Nancy W: *Influencing Hemingway: People and Places That Shaped His Life And Work*. Rowman and Littlefield 2014.

Spanier, Sandra and Trogdon, Robert W (eds): *The Letters of Ernest Hemingway* Volume 1, 1907–1922. Cambridge University Press, 2011.

Spanier, Sandra, DeFazio III, Albert J and Trogdon, Robert W(eds): *The Letters of Ernest Hemingway* Volume 2, 1923–1925. Cambridge University Press 2013.

Villard, Henry S, and Nagle, James: *Hemingway in Love and War, the Lost Diary of Agnes von Kurowsky*. Northeastern University Press, 1989.

Vittorini, Elio: *Conversations in Sicily*, translated by Alane
    Salierno Mason, Afterword by Ernest Hemingway. Canongate,
    Edinburgh 2003.
Wood, Naomi: *Mrs Hemingway*. Picador 2015.
Zorzi, Rosella Mamoli and Moriani, Gianni: *A Venezia e nel Veneto
    con Ernest Hemingway*. Supernova, Venice 2011.

Selected Articles

'Nacque a Taormina la prima opera del grande Ernest
    Hemingway': Sara Faraci, *tempostretto*, *quotidiano online di
    Messina e provincia*, 18 January 2013.
'Hemingway Debut in Italy in 1919': Giancarlo Cortese,
    L'ItaloEuropeo, 5 February 2013.
'Enough of a Bad Gamble: Correcting the Misinformation on
    Hemingway's Captain James Gamble': Gerry Brenner, *The
    Hemingway Review*, September 2000.
'The First Fine Careless Rapture': Peter Green, *The New Republic*,
    25 January 2012.
'The Forgotten Riviera': Georgina Gordon-Ham, *Rivista*, *magazine
    of the British-Italian Society*, No 396, 2013/14.
'La Casa di Hemingway': *Corriere del Veneto*, 27 August 2014.
'Quando Hemingway spiegava "Sono un ragazzo del Basso Piave"':
    Corriere della Sera, 26 April 2011.
'Hemingway Out of The Jungle, Arm Hurt, He Says Luck Holds':
    New York Times, 26 January 1954.
'Hemingway, il cacciatore che non aveva mira': *La Repubblica*, 20
    July 1999.
'Ernest Hemingway Letters Reveal Painful Years of Affection and
    Loss': *The Guardian*, 30 March 2012.

'Pilgrimage Variations, Hemingway's Sacred Landscapes': HR
    Stoneback, *Religion and Culture*, Vol 35 No 2/3, Summer–
    Autumn 2003, University of Notre Dame.

'The Nasty Mess, Hemingway, Italian Fascism and the New
    Review Controversy of 1932': Mark Cirino, *The Hemingway
    Review*, March 2014.

'Il Duce and Papa': Jennifer Theriault, *The American in Italia*,
    December 2011.

'Letters Home Reveal Another Side of Ernest Hemingway':
    Melissa Beattie-Moss, *Penn State News*, 8 September 2008.

'The Jilting of Ernest Hemingway': Scott Donaldson, *Virginia
    Quarterly Review*, Autumn 1989.

'Hemingway e il Friuli': Carlo Gaberscek, *La Cineteca di Friuli*,
    July 2005.

'Venezia e Hemingway, sulle orme di un mito letterario': Massimo
    Rozin, *Altritaliani.net*, 13 July 2014.

'Nel Veneto mio nonno Ernest Hemingway a diventato uomo,
    sperimentand': *Il Gazzettino*, 23 July 2015.

'Hemingway in Italy, Making It Up': Robert W Lewis, *Journal of
    Modern Literature*, Indiana University, Vol 9 No 2, 1982.

'Hemingway inedito, inizio un romanzo su D'Annunzio': *La
    Repubblica*, 3 April 1996.

'Quando Hemingway passo di qua', *Roncade.it*, 11 September 2013.

'Ernest Hemingway's "How Death Sought Out the Town Major
    of Roncade", Observations on the Development of a Writer':
    Matthew C. Stewart, *Literary Imagination*, Oxford, Vol 8 No 2,
    2006.

'Cercando la villa dove passo Hemingway': *La Domenica di
    Vicenza*, 16 January 2010.

'Being Ernest: John Walsh Unravels the Mystery Behind
    Hemingway's Suicide': *The Independent*, 10 June 2011.

'Hemingway on War and its Aftermath': Thomas Putnam, *Prologue Magazine*, US National Archives and Records Administration, Vol 38 No 1, 2006.

'Hemingway e mia sorella: la vera storia di un' amicizia'. *Il Giornale*, 23 November 2014.

'Ernest Hemingway's Long Ago Crush on a Venetian Girl is Once Again the Talk of Italy': Olghina di Robilant, *People Magazine*, 1 December 1980.

'La Piccola Guerra della Repubblica di San Marino': Enrico Silvestri, *Il Giornale*, 2 June 2013.

'Harry's Bar in Venice': Mary Hemingway, *Holiday Magazine*, June 1968.

'Hemingway and Guy Hickok in Italy – The Brooklyn Eagle Articles': Paul Montgomery, *The Hemingway Review*, 22 September 2005.

'And I Wasn't Dead Any More, One Story behind *A Farewell to Arms*': Rufus F, *Ordinary Times, ordinary-gentlemen.com*, 30 September 2014.

'Hemingway in the North East of Italy': *Yourizon*, Pordenone, May 2013.

'Personaggi d'Estate: Mario Berrino': Alain Elkann, *La Stampa*, 21 July 1999.

'"Hemingway e mia sorella": la vera storia di un'amicizia': Stefano Lorenzetto, *Il Giornale*, 23 November 2014.

'Hemingway: A Final Meeting with Adriana Ivancich at Nervi', Ann N Doyle and Neal B Houston, *The Hemingway Review*, Fall 1988.

'Talk with Mr Hemingway', Harvey Breit, *New York Times*, 17 September 1950.

'Piave, Papadopoli and Peace: The HAC in Italy, 1918', Justine Taylor, *Honourable Artillery Company Journal*, Vol 85 No 475, Autumn 2008.